Disrupting Grace

DISRUPTING

A STORY OF
Relinquishment
and Healing

Kristen Richburg

VMI Publishers • Sisters, Oregon

Published by
VMI Publishers
Sisters, Oregon
www.vmipublishers.com

ISBN: 1-935265-04-0

ISBN 13: 978-1-935265-04-7

Library of Congress: 2009937858

Printed in the USA

Cover design by Joe Bailen

TABLE *of* CONTENTS

Dedication

To Annie
Your example of gentle confidence and grace are an inspiration.

To Ben
Thank you for showing us all what unconditional love means.

Preface

I have two children. I used to have three. My third child didn't grow up and leave home; she didn't die. I relinquished her. I stood before a judge and said that I was no longer able to meet her needs. She is living with another family now and has a new last name.

For five years she called me "Mom." Now she calls someone else that. I don't know that I'll ever get used to it. I still wake up each day and go to bed at night asking myself, "How did I get here? Were those five years a dream?" Aren't adoption stories supposed to have happy endings?

While many adoption stories do have happy endings, this is not one of them. And I've come to learn that I am not alone. More and more families are finding themselves in situations similar to mine, feeling like there is no way out. There are people, experts even, who will tell you anyone can adopt. There are some who will tell you everyone should adopt a child, that if you can provide and there is a need, it's up to you to fulfill it.

What are families to do when despite all efforts, their child isn't thriving and the rest of the family is coming apart at the seams?

Sometimes I wish I could erase my adoption story. Most of the time I am thankful I can't. I know there was a purpose for all of it. And my life will never be the same.

A new story has begun.

CHAPTER ONE

Close Call

C ode Blue," the nurse said as she flew past me to flip the switch above my hospital bed. The room began to spin.

"I'm tired," I said. "I feel like I need to fall into a deep sleep."

The nurse waved my husband Andrew over. "Help us, please. Do everything you can to keep your wife awake." With our new son in his arms, he rushed to my side and slapped at my face. "Honey, stay awake. Don't go to sleep. Stay with us. Please don't go to sleep."

"Mr. Richburg, you need to leave the room."

Someone ushered him out, and he was gone. Suddenly there were half a dozen people on each side of my bed. One was there just to hold my hand, but it wasn't my husband. Where was he? Where had he gone? Thoughts swirled into my mind, but I couldn't make sense of any of it.

I was in pain. I had just given birth to our son—four weeks prior to my due date. I was feeling the relief of it being over when the pain returned. "What's happening to me?" I asked. There was no answer. I felt a sting, and heat rose up into my arm.

"We're hooking you up to fluids." Another sting. "We're going to give you some pain medication." I had no idea what had gone wrong. I waited for the drugs to kick in. *Did they give them to me? Why do I still hurt all over?* I began to cry and couldn't stop.

Meanwhile, Andrew was in the nursery, sent there to sit alone with our baby. He began to fear that he might be leaving the hospital a single parent. Our daughter, just thirteen months older than her brother, had spent the night with friends. The thought of going home and raising two children alone began to overwhelm him. He'd never imagined losing his wife like this. My brother Jon, who had been in the waiting room, was allowed to sit with him. They sat together in silence while my husband cried, fearing the worst.

Forty-five minutes later, it was over. As quickly as everyone had rushed in, they were gone. I was left alone in the room with the nurse. She checked my fluids and set me up to be monitored from her nurse's station, and then she was gone too.

My husband came back. He looked terrible. His eyes were red and swollen like mine, and we smiled through tears when we saw each other. It was over, and I was okay.

The next day the doctor visited our hospital room to tell us what had happened. She said that after our son was born, she was working to remove the placenta, the lifeline to my baby. It tore, and only a small part of it came out. Minutes later I began to hemorrhage. I lost a third of my total blood supply in less than a minute. When I said I was getting sleepy, I was really going into shock, possibly heading toward a coma.

"We needed to get that placenta out immediately. We had to scrape out your insides so we could stop the hemorrhaging. We tried to give you pain medication, but your blood pressure dropped, so we couldn't. We're sorry about that. We ran a test on your placenta. It was dead. Lucky for you, your baby knew it was time to come out. He was losing weight. Had you given birth on your due date, it's likely he wouldn't be here. It's fortunate you were in a hospital. Had you given birth anywhere else, you wouldn't be here today either."

Fast-forward two years. "Honey, I think we might want to think about having a third," one of us said to the other one day. We had always wanted three kids. Pregnancies had been hard on my body, and obviously my last delivery had been difficult. I called my OB. We chatted, getting caught up.

"How's Ben?" she asked.

"Doing well, thriving and healthy," I was happy to report. "So," I said,

"we're thinking of having another. Do you think my body can handle another pregnancy and delivery?"

There was a moment of silence. I said to her, "We are very open to adoption. I want you to be straight with me. I'm not hanging on you to say that we can do it. We'll adopt if you think it's too risky."

She explained that while she didn't want to say that we couldn't have any more children biologically, she wouldn't necessarily recommend it. "We'd watch you closely and consider you high risk. We'd do extra check-ups to monitor your progress. Your delivery would be scheduled, and we'd prepare for the worst. It's possible that if things went wrong, we'd need to do a full hysterectomy immediately following your delivery."

It was decided. We would adopt.

CHAPTER TWO

Anticipation

We began taking steps to learn about becoming adoptive parents. We read books, articles, anything we could get our hands on. There were things to consider. Should we pursue a domestic or international adoption? An infant? An older child? Which agency should we choose? We were excited about the possibilities, and we began the process of adopting at full speed.

We found an agency out of Oregon that could do the adoption part. We decided on international adoption. We requested a girl from Thailand. We had heard wonderful things about Thailand's foster care program. It was important to us that our daughter not be institutionalized, but rather be living in a loving home, part of a family. I myself am an international adoptee from Korea. It seemed like the right fit.

At the time, we were living in Minnesota. We found an agency there to do our in-state home study. We worked hard to put together our home study and our dossier, which included a written essay describing our family life, our childhoods, and our parenting philosophies. It also included legal documents, criminal records, our financial information…you name it. If it was information about us, it was in there. The whole process was amazingly detailed and time-consuming, but we were so excited to be moving forward that we worked quickly to get our paperwork in.

Adoption is a process of "hurry up and wait." After making multiple copies and sending off paperwork to all the necessary recipients, we began to wait. And wait.

In the meantime, I regularly visited our Oregon agency's Web site. It featured an online forum where adoptive parents from all over the world posted questions, comments, or news about their adoption stories. It was thrilling to read. Many were ahead of us in the process and were getting referrals or had finally been issued travel dates. Others wrote about bringing their child home. The stories were filled with joy, celebration, and hope. It was a reminder to us that we weren't waiting alone and that soon enough we would have our own celebration story to share.

Months later we received our referral. Our social worker called to tell us we could come to the agency at our earliest convenience to pick up our daughter's paperwork and pictures. Andrew and I rushed to the agency, barely able to focus on the road. We were shaking with anticipation. The agency knew we were excited, so they didn't delay. They handed us the papers as we entered the building.

The first thing we searched for were the pictures. There were several of them. We were elated to see her: she was absolutely darling, and we fell in love with her instantly. The first picture was of our baby in the hospital, taken sometime within the first few weeks of her life. She was tiny, wearing a bodysuit, with jet black hair that seemed to stick out in all directions and eyes wide open. Her head was turned a little sideways, making it difficult to see her entire face.

The second picture was of her sitting in a wicker-type chair outside. The picture was taken at a distance, so the image was smaller than the first. She was sitting up in the chair, smiling, wearing an orange outfit. Her hair, just above her ears, was parted on the side and combed. Although the image was small, she had a very cute look about her, and we were taken with her smile. The third and last picture was labeled "Thirteen months." Our soon-to-be daughter was sitting on what looked to be the concrete floor of a house. There was nothing around her to give us an idea of what her home life was like. She was dressed in a pink dress, hair parted and combed, looking at the camera. No smile was present on her face. She looked tiny in that empty room. Tiny, and maybe even a little…sad. It was hard to tell, as the picture was not completely clear.

Andrew and I sat for a while staring at the pictures, hugging each other. Then we began to read. There was information about our daughter's birth mother and extended family. Our "baby" was already thirteen months old. We hurried home to share the pictures with our children, who were waiting for us with a sitter.

For weeks after seeing those pictures for the first time, I imagined holding our daughter in that pink dress, her tiny figure in my arms. It saddened me to think that she was already thirteen months old and that every day we waited was another day without her. I could hardly stand it that we were missing those days of holding her and watching her grow.

Annie and Ben, who were four and three at the time, couldn't wait to meet their new sister. They talked with us about names, things they couldn't wait to show her, things they wanted to teach her. We decided to name her Emma. We prayed for her every day. We prayed for her protection. We prayed that her foster family was showering love upon her as we so much wanted to do ourselves. We prayed for her safety. And we prayed for her grief. We were certain that once we went to get her, she would face enormous sadness at leaving the only family she knew to come live with ours.

What will she be like? What will she look like by the time we get to meet her? What makes her smile, laugh? What makes her cry? We pondered these things while we prepared for her long-awaited arrival. Emma would likely come home in the fall or early winter. Coming from Thailand, where the average temperature year-round was ninety degrees, we knew she'd be unprepared for Minnesota winters. We had fun shopping for her, stocking up on sweaters, flannel pajamas, hats and mittens. We bought matching bedding for her and Annie, who couldn't wait to share her room with her little sister. Her closet was full, her room was ready…we were more than ready!

During this time we also met with a therapist in town who worked with adopted children and their families, more specifically, on attachment-related issues. I have a degree in social work. My husband has a master's degree in special education. We wanted to be as prepared and knowledgeable as possible about issues we might face with Emma. We talked about how to best help Emma transition and deal with her grief.

At last the phone call came. Could we be ready to leave in a few days?

"Absolutely!" we assured our agency. We scrambled to book flights, arrange care for Annie and Ben, pack up our things, and head off on our unforgettable adventure. We wrote letters to the kids that they could open each day while we were gone. We made a gigantic map for them so they could follow our route and see where we were going. We left detailed instructions for grandparents who would be caring for them.

The night before we left, Andrew and I had the house to ourselves. We'd dropped the kids at my parents' house earlier that day. Thailand is twelve hours ahead, so we stayed up most of the night to get ourselves acclimated to the time change. We were in celebration mode. We cranked up music and danced around the house. We were pumped with adrenaline and were motivated to tackle some projects. I suppose you could say we were nesting. We emptied and organized our front hall closet. We completely cleaned out our basement storage room. While going through boxes, we found love letters we had written to each other during our college days. We read through every one of them that night. We were filled with warm memories from our dating days, and with that combined with the excitement we were feeling about leaving for Thailand, we were bursting with joy. We set our alarm to wake us after just a couple of hours of sleep. There was no need to press the snooze button that morning. We were ready to go!

We traveled a long way to meet Emma. Thailand is literally on the other side of the world. Having our other children, we'd experienced the excitement of bringing a child home. We knew this would be different—bringing our little girl home from somewhere so far away—but nothing could have prepared us for how different it all would be.

After twenty-nine hours of travel, including a layover in Seattle and another in Tokyo, we arrived in Bangkok, Thailand, around two o'clock in the morning. We were tired, but still our hearts were racing.

We had heard that Bangkok was the "city that never sleeps." What an accurate description! We hurried outside the airport to catch a cab to the hotel. It was still about eighty degrees, and the humidity was near 100 percent. Our hotel was right in the heart of downtown. "Rush hour" couldn't begin to describe the congestion of Bangkok at 2 A.M. The traffic was terrible. We inched our way into the city to see that the number of cars on the road was nothing compared to the masses of people covering every side street and sidewalk. People were everywhere; children too. It was like a block party without the party.

The taxi windows were open, and the smell grew intense as we approached the crowded downtown streets. Street vendors were selling all sorts of delicacies, with several vendors crammed onto every block. The smell of garbage that had sat out in the sun too long was overwhelming.

We sat in silence in the car, our eyes like saucers. We checked our clocks again. Was it really 2 A.M.?

Our hotel was modern, surprisingly very American-like. We checked in and dragged ourselves up to our room. Exhausted, we fell into bed and drifted off to sleep.

CHAPTER THREE

Introductions

A ndrew and I both slept well, and we woke up feeling refreshed and ready for the day. We'd been sent our itinerary for the week before leaving the States, so we were prepared—so long as things went according to plan. We were to spend the morning at the hotel.

As we headed downstairs for breakfast, we were standing in the elevator when an American-looking couple walked in with a young Asian girl who appeared to be around seven years old. We struck up a conversation and learned that they were another family adopting through the same agency. We immediately bonded over the excitement we were feeling about meeting our Thai children sometime later that day. This was their second adoption. The young girl with them was their first child, adopted from China. This time they were adopting a son.

We went to the hotel restaurant together and spent the breakfast hour getting to know each other. They were dear people, and we enjoyed hearing the story of their first adoption. It was a wonderful experience, they said, and they were thrilled to be in Thailand adopting again. This was all so new to us, and being with them gave us comfort.

After breakfast, we were scheduled to meet our Thai social worker in one of the ballrooms. The room was set up with rows of chairs and a small platform in front. We met a third family, also from the States, who were there to adopt a boy. After quick introductions, our social worker stepped onto the platform and introduced herself. She was a pleasant woman with a warm, friendly smile, small in stature as was typical of many Thai women. She handed each of us an envelope, explaining that the paperwork inside contained the final updates from our foster families describing our children's social, emotional, and physical development.

We were all familiar with the papers, as we had been receiving updates like these over the past several months. This update, like the ones sent before, indicated that Emma was doing well, on target developmentally in every way. Once everyone reviewed their papers, we were told the children were already in the hotel and ready to meet us. All eyes in the room lit up, and we looked at each other in surprise. Did we hear her correctly? Emma was here? We'd had no idea that during the meeting Emma was just rooms away.

"If you are ready, we can move to the meeting room," the social worker said. *Here we go!*

We were sent to another ballroom, this one completely void of furniture. There were toys scattered throughout the room. We were told to sit on the floor, finding our own space among the toys so each family could be introduced to their child with as little distraction as possible. Andrew and I found a place on the floor by a wall of windows, a comfortable distance from the other families. When everyone was seated, the social worker stepped out into the hallway and signaled to her coworkers to bring the children in. Our hearts were pounding, my palms were sweaty, and I felt shaky to the core.

One by one, the children came in. It was a surreal moment when Emma appeared in the doorway. We couldn't believe it. Two years of work, time, waiting, and prayers had led up to this moment. She toddled in wide-eyed, looking gleeful. She was wearing a pink sundress we had sent her weeks earlier and a pair of worn blue Mickey Mouse sandals. Her hair was in a tiny bun near the top of her head. She had an engaging smile and curious nature. Her eye caught the toys on the floor, and without hesitating, she walked all the way into the center of the room.

The social worker who had come in with Emma took her by the hand and led her to us. She told Emma in Thai that we were her mommy and daddy.

Introductions

"Sawatdee ha," we said to Emma, our smiles trying to communicate more to her than our words could. *Sawatdee*, which means *hello*, completed our knowledge of the Thai language.

Emma put her hands together in a proper Thai greeting but did not respond with any words. She continued to survey the toys as we attempted to initiate play with her using gestures and smiles. She didn't say a word, although at times she let out a high-pitched, nervous-sounding giggle. She wasn't the least bit shy, but rather quite outgoing, enjoying the focused attention we were giving her. We took pictures and continued to play.

I looked over to the other families. They too were engaged in play, making silly faces and hand gestures like us. Time passed quickly, and after a while the social worker announced it was time to go to lunch. We'd eat in the hotel, she said, before the children would leave to return to their foster homes.

Lunch was animated and fun. We ate together with the other families, everyone beaming with excitement and joy. Emma sat on my lap. She didn't eat much, but she seemed very content. Content for now, I was sure, because she hadn't yet realized that in just two days, she'd be saying goodbye to her foster family forever. I was caught up in the enjoyment of the day, and yet my heart ached for her upcoming loss.

The children left immediately following lunch, and we were told we would meet up with them again the next morning for a shopping excursion. Andrew and I returned to our room, chatting nonstop. Wasn't she cute? Did you hear that laugh of hers? What a little thing she is!

On and on, we talked about everything we had noticed about her: her bright smile, her charming and playful personality. It was strange, too, how much we didn't know about her yet. There was much about her that was unfamiliar, that would take time getting to know, and she was already almost two years old. We spent the rest of the afternoon shopping in the city and exploring. We continued to talk throughout the day's event, eagerly anticipating the next day's outing.

It took a moment to remember where I was when I awoke the next morning, but as soon as I remembered, I was filled with anticipation. We took the elevator down to the hotel restaurant for breakfast, met up with

21

the other families from our agency, and chatted through breakfast, everyone sharing their reactions to the introductions the day before and voicing their excitement about the upcoming events.

After breakfast, we met up with the children and the social workers and headed to a local mall for an outing. We were excited to see Emma again. She showed up wearing another sundress we had sent her. This one was blue and covered with little flowers. Her hair was again in a little bun, and she had her Mickey Mouse sandals on. We could tell her sandals were too small for her feet, so we decided to find her a new pair of shoes during our shopping excursion. We walked around, had fun riding the escalator up and down, and bought Emma a new pair of sandals and a pink pair of regular shoes. We ate lunch at a restaurant in the mall and then made our way back to the hotel. We were told to nap the kids in our rooms and to meet up in the lobby in a couple of hours.

I was nervous about having Emma nap in our room. It was the first time we had broken off from the group to be alone with her. I wondered if she would panic and become upset and confused. I knew we wouldn't be able to comfort her or reassure her with words she would understand.

To our surprise, she had no problem coming with us to our room. On the contrary, she seemed perfectly fine. We brought her in, changed her diaper, and laid her down on the bed. We turned the lights off. There was nowhere to go, so we sat on the floor in the dark and waited in silence to see what she would do. Amazingly, within a few minutes, she closed her eyes and fell asleep.

We couldn't believe it. We tried to imagine our other kids doing that. If we had sent either one of them at twenty-two months to spend a day with strangers, strangers who didn't speak their language no less, and then to a hotel room to nap, they would have been hysterical—at least crying and confused. One of the other family's rooms was right below ours. We could hear their son crying and screaming through the floor of our room. He didn't let up for the entire two hours. That's what we had been told to be prepared for. And here our little girl was peacefully sleeping on our bed.

When she awoke, she was groggy, but ready to be on the go again. We met up with the other families in the lobby. Both of the other families looked exhausted. The two boys had screamed and cried throughout nap time, and they looked worn out too.

Emma, on the other hand, appeared happy and rested.

CHAPTER FOUR

Questions

The morning over, we split up and were taken by car to visit our children's foster families. Emma's social worker came with us to be our translator during our visit. On the way, she reminded us to be prepared for this meeting. Many of the foster families, she said, had grown attached to these children and would experience deep grief and sadness over saying good-bye.

What a gift this family has given, I thought, *to Emma and to us*. I could-n't wait to meet them and express how much their love and care had meant to us.

Emma's foster family lived an hour outside of Bangkok. As we drove, we took in the sights of the city and then the landscape as we got farther away from the hustle and bustle of downtown. Emma sat on my lap throughout the drive, content to sit still and feel the wind on her face com-ing in through the windows. When we were ten minutes away, the move-ment of the car lulled her to sleep. I moved to hold her in my arms so she could lie back. She slept in my arms for the last few minutes of our ride.

Inside, I was thrilled to be holding Emma, sleeping in my arms for the first time, and yet I was beginning to feel a little uneasy. When would she show her sadness and confusion? Did she really know what was hap-pening to her?

We turned onto a long dirt road with several houses on one side. *House* is perhaps not the correct word for these structures. They had makeshift walls—some had four, some only three. There were scraps of metal used for roofs, and the yards surrounding the homes were littered with heaping piles of garbage. A fire was burning outside one of the homes, and two children were playing with it. One child couldn't have been older than three.

A few chickens ran across the road in front of us. We came to the last house on the street: Emma's home. This house did have four walls and a roof. There were cutouts in the walls for windows—no glass or screens, just open spaces. We had been told that the rains were heavy over the past season and there had been some flooding in the area. A walkway to the house was covered with wooden palettes to step on. During the wet season, the palettes served to keep feet dry up to the house.

Emma woke up in my arms as we approached the door. I set her down, and she wandered inside. In the doorway we were introduced to Emma's foster mother and father, along with their adopted daughter, who looked to be around eight years old.

We entered the house and were taken aback by what we saw. The main living room was completely empty. The floor was cement and bare. We never saw any furniture, kitchen, bed, or sleeping mat of any kind. After introductions we all sat down, on the floor of course, and studied one another for a brief minute. Emma toddled around and appeared matter-of-fact that she had come home. Her foster parents behaved like that too. There was no warm, joyful reunion after having been apart for the day.

Emma's foster parents looked to be in their mid-forties. Both of them had faces that were dark and weathered, almost leathery. Ma, as Emma called her, wore a simple blue dress that resembled an old-fashioned housecoat, hanging loosely over her body with the hem hanging just above the floor. I can't recall what name Emma used for her foster father. He had a friendly smile and wore a plain, cream-colored linen shirt and dark slacks.

Our meeting with Emma's foster family gave us a chance to ask questions about Emma and their experience with her. We had many questions about her routine life in Thailand. We hoped to be able to replicate much of what was familiar to her to provide initial comfort during the early stages of transitioning. Our social worker translated.

"We are hoping you could answer some questions for us about Emma," we said. "What are her favorite activities?"

With little expression, Ma gave a brief response.

"She likes to play," the social worker said.

"What are Emma's favorite foods?"

"She eats about anything," came the translation.

"Does she have a toy or blanket she is most attached to? When she is sad, how do you comfort her?" we asked.

Again, without animation or expression, Ma answered matter-of-factly, "No, she doesn't have a favorite toy. I don't know; I just hold her when she's sad."

Ma gave Emma a bottle and sat Emma on her lap. As the conversation continued to dry up, Emma wriggled her way out of Ma's lap until she was on her back on the hard floor. She took most of her bottle that way. Hiding my look of surprise, I realized that Emma's behavior was not out of the ordinary for them.

Ma answered all of our questions with general or vague responses. Is she shy, I wondered, or are we putting her on the spot and she's uncomfortable? She looked strangely removed and distant, quiet unless questioned. Emma's foster father didn't say a word, just smiled at us from time to time whenever we looked at him.

Where is the grief we were told to be prepared for? Where are the stories about Emma, the specifics? Perhaps Emma's foster parents were trying to emotionally protect themselves. *They must be sad to see Emma go, but are trying to be strong for her and for us,* I was sure.

Our time was running out.

"We want to express our appreciation to you for taking care of our daughter," Andrew said as we opened the bag of gifts we had for them. Looking at Emma's foster father, Andrew presented him with a watch. "We hope this serves as a reminder of your time caring for Emma. We will never forget what you've done for her."

Emma's foster father took the watch with a nod and a smile, saying "Thank you," in Thai.

I looked at Ma. I held out a carved wooden angel titled, "Angel of Protection."

"Words cannot express our gratitude and appreciation for you. We consider you Emma's angel of protection because you have cared for her and loved her for us. Thank you again, so very much."

She too smiled and said "Thank you" in Thai. An awkward moment of silence followed as our social worker signaled for us to say our good-byes.

We walked outside and said good-bye to Emma and her foster family, hoping they understood our deep level of appreciation. I couldn't have known at the time that the irony of those gifts and what they symbolized would later come back and fill us with regret.

Emma would be brought to the hotel the next morning, and then she would officially be ours. Our driver brought us back to the hotel, where we bumped into the other families in the lobby. They had just returned from their visits. Everyone shared stories of the afternoon. The two other families had had wonderful visits. Both of the other foster families were painfully sad over parting with their foster kids. One family had invited all of their extended family to the meeting, and many of them were crying. The other foster families were full of stories about the children, and were excited and animated in sharing them with the new adoptive parents. There wasn't enough time, they said, to get it all in. It was clear these foster families had really bonded with the boys, and it was heartbreaking to see them go.

"How was your visit?" they asked.

To be honest, after hearing their stories, I felt a little deflated.

"It was fine," we said. We went on to tell them how it went, that we felt strange about the meeting and somewhat confused. Our new friends tried to be reassuring.

"Maybe they are really sad over Emma leaving, but they just aren't comfortable showing it. They may have distanced themselves from Emma recently so the good-byes won't be so difficult."

questions

We thanked everyone for being so encouraging and hoped they were right. Something inside us, however, wasn't so convinced.

Everyone headed back to their hotel rooms to decompress. We went upstairs, dropped our bags, and got ready for dinner. Once in the room, Andrew and I were unusually quiet, too distracted with thought to have a conversation. We looked at each other knowingly, both of us trying to manage feelings of concern, fearful of doubt. I saw in Andrew's eyes the same feeling I had, the relief that we had each other. I knew we would talk at dinner, but for now the time we had alone with our thoughts was needed.

It was past the dinner hour, and the sun had already set. We were told it wouldn't be wise to wander the streets of Bangkok after dark. Instead, we ate a late dinner in the hotel restaurant.

After our food arrived, we began to discuss the day. It had been full and exhausting, with so much to process. The shopping experience had been fun. Emma loved riding the escalators. Nap time had been unbelievably easy. Soon, our conversation turned to Emma's foster family. Thoughts about that meeting weighed heavily on our minds. It seemed strange, even bizarre, that it was so difficult to get any specific information from them. Were they just reserved and shy? Or was there something they weren't telling us? We didn't know. And why did they seem so unaffected by our meeting and Emma's soon departure?

Conversation ceased, the two of us lost in the details of the day and contemplating what to do. We watched out the window as people rushed by, as the city prepared itself for another sleepless night. Vendors repositioned their carts, and traffic was still moving at a mad, frantic pace. For the first time since arriving in Thailand, we felt lost.

"Is there anything we can do? I asked. "I mean, do you think we could talk to the social worker about this?"

"I don't know," Andrew replied. "I think we can share our concerns with her. She may be able to tell us something we don't know about Emma's foster family. If nothing else, I'd feel better knowing we did our best to be as informed as possible."

We walked back up to our room, the worries of the day slowing our steps. I couldn't wait to crawl into bed. Sleep, however, was slow to come. I played out the scene of meeting Emma's foster family over and over again in my mind. I tried to remember every expression, smile, word spoken. Was there something we had missed? Did Emma seem happy and secure with her family? What would we say to the social worker? I got out of bed and fished out a Tylenol PM from my cosmetic bag, wishing I had taken one sooner.

As the minutes passed into morning, my ability to reason and surrender my worries had slowly diminished. Anxiety had taken hold as I wrestled with my thoughts and against what I believed to be true. We were in the right place. God had brought us here and to Emma. He knew what He was doing, and trusting Him was all that was required of me. As the Tylenol began to take its effect, I finally felt myself drifting off to sleep.

∞

After a fitful night's sleep and a quick breakfast the next morning, we readied ourselves for Emma's arrival at the hotel. She was saying her good-byes at home and would not see her foster family again. We had taken time that morning to unpack the goodies we had brought for her: toys, a stuffed dog from Annie and Ben, a new blanket, and a few new outfits were among the things we'd been waiting to give her.

After breakfast, we met up with the other families in the lobby. We visited with each other while waiting for the children. The head social worker called for everyone's attention and reviewed our itinerary. After the children had arrived, we'd taxi to the Thai Consulate for an interview and for government approval to move ahead with adoption. It was just a formality, she said. This was the government's opportunity to ensure that these children were going to safe homes. Then we would move on to the American Embassy, where we'd receive Emma's visa for travel to the United States.

Everyone was prepared for the meetings. We had been instructed to wear appropriate clothing: men in dress pants and tie, women in dresses or skirts. Each of us wanted to look our best for those important meetings. The group chatted nervously while we watched for the agency van to pull up outside.

The head social worker pulled us aside. She knew that I had been adopted years ago, also through the agency in Oregon.

"Would you be willing to speak to my colleagues this afternoon about your experience growing up in the States? Your story would be helpful to us as we work with adoptive parents, helping prepare them to raise an adopted child. We could go straight to the Thai branch agency after our appointment at the Embassy."

I looked to Andrew, who seemed to shrug, "Why not?"

"Sure," I replied. "I'd be happy to." As I looked at Andrew again, we sensed instantly what the other was thinking. The opportunity we were hoping for, to talk to the social worker, had just fallen into our laps. *Thank you, Lord.*

∞

No sooner had we made the plan than the agency van pulled up outside the hotel. We could see the children getting out with their social workers. Each of them had a small bag of belongings. Emma was still taking a bottle, so her social worker also carried a small diaper bag filled with diapers, bottles, and formula. When they arrived in the lobby, we all stood together for pictures. We took several group photos of the three families with our children and the social workers too. Everyone was smiling ear to ear. It was going to be a memorable day!

Gathering up our belongings, we hailed cabs and made our way to the Thai Consulate. Everything went smoothly. Each family had a turn to meet with the government officials. Questions included everything from "Describe your home" to "If your child would like to return to Thailand one day, will you allow it? Will you educate your child about her heritage?" They were easy questions, but our desire to do well and make a good impression kept our nerves up until the interview was over.

We made it to the Embassy shortly thereafter and waited in queue for our visas. Again, things went smoothly, and before long the official for-malities were over.

We caught a cab with the social worker to the Thai agency. The event ended up being a bit more than I had expected. I spoke to a group of around thirty people, answering questions about my experience as an adopted child. The whole thing took about an hour. At the end, the agency presented me with a large wooden clock as a gift.

Before leaving, everyone walked us outside for a group picture and to say good-bye. Months after we arrived home, the agency sent me our inter-view printed up in a local Thai newspaper. A picture of Andrew, me, and Emma was also included in the article. I have no idea what it said since it was written in Thai, but it made for a good story!

On the way back to the hotel in the taxi, we knew our opportunity had arrived to voice our concerns about Emma to the social worker. We had several. First, Emma didn't speak. At all, not even in Thai. At twenty-two months, we considered that unusual. She seemed developmentally behind in many ways. We asked about that. The social worker told us that Emma was one of several children who had come out of that foster home. The agency had observed that the children coming out of that home were typically behind. She gave no reason why, just that they'd seen it before. Concerning Emma's speech, she told us not to worry. Emma's hearing had been checked, and she was fine. Some kids just start speak-ing late.

Second on our list of concerns was Emma's foster family. We described our visit with them. She said what we had hoped to hear: that some fam-ilies distance themselves at the end because saying good-bye can be emo-tionally hard. She was sure Emma had been in good care, so again, not to worry.

Finally, we asked, why was Emma so happy? Why wasn't she grieving or showing any signs of sadness about losing her foster family? The other kids had been very emotional from day one, one boy just thirteen months and the other five years old. Both boys had been inconsolable at times, especially that day as they met with the government officials and got their visas at the Embassy. Emma, on the other hand, had been fine, content to be along for the outings with us— people she didn't know and who didn't speak her language.

The social worker tried to reassure us that some children don't grieve while still in Thailand. Some will grieve instead once they've arrived in the States. She told us to be prepared for that. Grief can show itself in many ways. She said to be ready for inconsolable long periods of sadness, crying, anger or rage, illness, or vomiting.

We were glad to have had a chance to talk with her, but we wished her attempts to reassure us had been more successful. We tried our best to believe her, and we clung to her words, hoping she was right.

CHAPTER FIVE

Welcome Home

Back at the hotel, Emma napped for us and woke up happy. We were on our own for good now, each family spending time getting to know their children. We spent the time until dinner walking around the hotel, riding the elevators, and walking some more. Emma loved it. We took her to dinner where she ate most of her food. She was obsessed with the stairs that led into the restaurant—stairs were a completely new thing for her, it seemed. After many times of going up and down, it was all we could do to pull her away from them. It was time to get her back to the room and ready for bed.

We gave her a bath and put her in a new pair of pajamas. We handed her the new stuffed puppy that Annie and Ben had sent for us to give her. She didn't know what to do with it. She looked at it in her hand and then let go, dropping it to the floor. We gave it to her again, hugging it first and holding it, showing her what to do. She had a completely blank look on her face as she again let it drop to the floor. She did the same thing with a picture book we handed to her. It was as if she'd never seen anything like it before. We looked at the picture book together and sang her a couple of songs, then laid her down. Within minutes she was sleeping.

We called the kids that night. It was morning in Minnesota, so they were busy in their morning routine with breakfast and getting ready for the day. We had been through so much emotionally over the past few days, it was wonderful to hear their voices. We missed them terribly. We told them all about our time, and about Emma. We wanted to get caught up on what they had been doing while we were gone. They'd been having a good time with grandparents and were ready for us to come home. We couldn't wait to get there. Although we hadn't been gone that long, we felt homesick and emotionally spent.

With Emma sleeping soundly, we began to pack our things. Our travel time home would be somewhere near twenty-two hours, shorter than our flight out due to one less layover on our return route. We laid out two warm outfits for Emma, socks, and her new shoes. We put out our travel clothes, and I laid out a backup outfit for myself as well. We'd heard many stories of families traveling home and children getting very sick on flights. We made sure Emma's diaper bag was packed with bottles, formula, diapers, and lots of wipes in case she should be sick on the plane.

We were thrilled about going home! We couldn't wait to begin life together as a family of five. We dug into the hotel minibar and helped ourselves to Toblerone chocolate and potato chips. We felt giddy as we danced around the room in silence for fear of waking Emma. Our celebration came to an end when we ran out of chocolate.

The travel home was remarkably uneventful. Emma slept most of the way, which we viewed to be a miracle. We were exhausted by the time we touched ground and worked our way through customs, but our excitement to see Annie and Ben kicked in, and we were feeling more awake by the minute. After leaving the customs room, we headed out through sliding doors to the international baggage claim area.

Annie and Ben, along with our parents, my brothers and their families, and many friends were there, waiting to welcome us off the plane. It was November 8, 2002, and Emma was home! It was wonderful to see so many familiar faces. We have many pictures from that time and are so thankful for the support our family and friends demonstrated to us on that day.

It took a few days to get over jet lag. Andrew's parents were staying with us from out of town, and they were helpful in helping us get back to routine. They made meals for us and folded the laundry. They played with

Annie and Ben when we needed to attend to Emma.

We watched and waited for Emma to show some sign or indication that the transition was stressful for her in some way. After all, her entire world had just been turned upside down. She was surrounded by new sights and sounds, and not a single face or voice was familiar to her. We kept hearing our social worker's words in our heads, reminding us to be prepared for uncontrollable grief, sickness, or rage.

But Emma did not display any of these characteristics—rather the opposite. She was too happy, slept easily, never cried. All of these things might sound like she was making a nice transition, but with our background knowledge regarding issues of attachment and the information we had received from the therapist before our trip, we had a good inclination that something wasn't right. She showed little to no sign of being affected by anything. She had a glazed-over look about her, masked by a frozen smile. There was no eye contact, no expressed grief, no sign of fear.

Weeks passed by. Emma continued to eat and sleep well, and we were doing our best to show her the boundaries and rules of our home. We spent a lot of time on the floor just playing with the kids. Emma was getting used to the cold weather too. We played outside as the days grew shorter and colder that first month. Most of the leaves had fallen off the trees, and the kids enjoyed jumping in the raked piles in the backyard. Emma tried swinging on swings and going down slides for the first time. She needed some lessons on simple things, like how to play and how to imitate. She clearly didn't know what to do with toys of almost any kind. We'd hug a stuffed animal, then hand it to her and gesture to her that it was her turn. She'd give us that blank look, the same one she had made in the hotel in Thailand. We made sounds, faces, or actions like clapping our hands, trying to get her to imitate. Nothing. She looked confused and unable to understand what it was we were trying to get her to do.

We were a bit confused ourselves about what we thought about her transition so far. The grieving we had hoped for hadn't yet come. She still seemed very behind developmentally, almost infant-like, despite her early progress reports from the agency that said she was developmentally on track. We wondered if maybe she was just in a numb state, or if she had regressed due to all the changes she'd been through. Still, we thought, once she became more comfortable with us, she'd begin to show her true self.

Early in December, ladies from our Sunday-school class wanted to throw a shower for Emma to celebrate her arrival. A couple of my girl-friends hosted the event, and my mom and sisters-in-law were there too. I brought Emma with me so I could introduce her to everyone. Andrew planned on picking her up after the first thirty minutes so that he could get her home and put her to bed. Because Emma wasn't our first child, I'd made a request for no gifts, but indicated on the invitation that attendees could bring a small child's gift to be donated to the Thailand foster care program. Remembering how little Emma's foster family had, we hoped that gifts donated would end up with foster families like hers.

It was a nice evening. Emma spent her time running back and forth to different ladies and giving them hugs. She loved being the center of attention and put on quite a show. Everyone thought it was cute. Her indiscriminate friendliness, however, stressed me out, and I was ready for her to go when Andrew showed up. The ladies asked me to share the story of meeting Emma, and I brought a small clip from the videotape we'd made in Thailand to show everyone.

I was still slightly anxious about Emma and was struggling to feel relieved and thankful, but I tried to put my worries aside for the evening and focus on the "thankful" part. Everyone brought gifts to be donated to the agency. Later that week we boxed them up and sent them to the agency in Oregon. I called ahead to let them know the box was coming and communicate our desire to have it sent on to the Thailand branch to be distributed to foster families. I never heard from the agency with any response, nor did I ever have a chance to find out what happened to the gifts.

CHAPTER SIX

Attachment 101

That same month, we brought Emma to the International Adoption Clinic at the University of Minnesota. They gave her a full physical exam. Because they specialize in seeing children from other countries, they took greater care in checking for signs or symptoms typical of kids coming from overseas. Emma was physically healthy, although small. They also did an evaluation of her emotional state. Their assessment of her was that she seemed emotionally unattached, and they recommended we seek guidance to help facilitate her attachment to us. Coincidentally, they referred us to the therapist we'd seen before leaving for Thailand. We told them we'd met with him before and would follow up with getting Emma in to see him.

Christmas was coming. We set up our Christmas tree, filled it with lights, and watched as Annie and Ben had fun decorating it. Emma seemed unaffected by it all. She wasn't interested in the tree, and she didn't seem to notice the decorations. It was a busy time, and the days blurred together. It was our turn to be with my side of our extended family, and this year it was planned that after Christmas we'd all be together in Florida for a week. We'd had some concerns about taking Emma so soon after getting home, but we thought it would be fine since we'd all be together.

A couple of days before our trip, we set out our suitcases to pack. I'd nearly finished packing the kids' clothes when Emma started acting strangely. By bedtime she was screaming and crying. When I tried to hold her, she arched her back and closed her eyes. She was out of sorts, and we couldn't calm her down. We were at a loss about what to do—and then it hit me. The last time she'd seen our suitcases, we were in Thailand, packing to come home. Was this her first sign of grief over leaving Thailand? It was difficult trying to help her, and yet Andrew and I both felt some relief that Emma might finally be at the beginning stages of grieving her loss. We got her to bed after trying in vain to console her. We wondered that night what the next day of travel would hold and what emotional state Emma might be in.

We left early the next day for the airport. Emma was quiet, but not visibly upset. Once we got to the airport, she blew out her diaper. It was a mess. We got her cleaned up and into a second change of clothes. Her diarrhea continued throughout the plane ride. It seemed like as soon as we'd get her cleaned up, another blowout would occur. By the time we landed, Emma was wearing nothing but a diaper and a T-shirt. There was nothing left in her stomach but acid, and her little body kept shooting it out. The smell was terrible, beyond any soiled diaper I'd ever experienced. She blew out her last diaper in the rental-car parking lot while sitting in her stroller. We donated the stroller to the car- rental agency!

Was Emma continuing to grieve, we wondered throughout that travel day? We remembered the social worker saying that kids can get physically sick with grief that can last for days. We didn't have to wait any longer for our answer. As soon as we arrived at the place where we were staying, Emma was a new girl. She bolted inside, screaming and laughing, full of energy. She ran from room to room, looking into each one, and came out looking delighted and happy. Her stomach was instantly better too. It seemed that once Emma realized we were somewhere new and still all together, she could relax. It occurred to me later that Emma might have assumed when we were packing up our suitcases that we were taking her back to Thailand. When she figured out we hadn't taken her there, she was giddy and joyful.

For the next four years, every time we traveled, Emma's stomach was upset, usually causing her to vomit the day or night before leaving town and often en route to our destination. No matter how many times we'd try to reassure her of where we were going and that we'd all be together, it wouldn't be until we'd arrive that she could settle down. She made progress, though. In the fifth year, she was able to see suitcases without screaming and crying, and she was finally able to conquer trips without incident or an upset stomach.

We had a nice time in Florida. The kids enjoyed the beach and playing outside, glad to be in the warm weather away from our cold Minnesota winter. It ended all too quickly, and soon we were back home, settling into routine again.

∞

"It's Annie's turn to sit in my lap. You are going to have to wait. It will be your turn next." I could barely hear myself speak over Emma's screams. Annie had just taken a fall and had come to me for comfort and a hug. Emma clawed at Annie and scratched at my hands, screaming. Annie looked up at me with confusion mixed with sadness. I left her for a moment to take Emma to another room.

"If you cannot wait your turn without screaming, you will wait in here until Annie's done."

Emma continued to scream even after I closed the door. She went on for another few minutes until she realized she no longer had an audience and gave it up.

So far, Emma had not turned out to be the little sister the kids had hoped she'd be. They had imagined a sweet girl who would look up to them and want to do what they did. Annie had waited for a little sister to share her room. A couple of weeks after Emma's arrival, we realized that her sharing a room with Annie was not an option. Ben gave up his room for Emma, and he moved into Annie's. We thought it would only be for a while.

I went back to get Emma a few minutes later, after Annie was feeling better.

"Thank you for waiting. It's your turn now." I headed back to the couch, sat down, and put out my arms. Emma walked toward me, looked me in the eyes, then ran off. It took many instances like this one until I began to realize that Emma never really wanted a turn; she just didn't want Annie or Ben to have one. If I showed affection to either of them in any way, Emma would be right there, scratching and hitting the kids, screaming in their faces. She screamed at me too, demanding my focus be on her.

We tried to teach her that everyone got a turn at our house, but time and again, when it was her turn or when positive attention or affection were given to her, she made it clear that she didn't want anything to do with it. It was a crazy-feeling, push-pull relationship. When we'd try to connect with her, she'd refuse. When we weren't connecting with her, she demanded we drop what we were doing to focus on her—not connect with her, but give her our full attention.

It became obvious early on that Annie and Ben were viewed by Emma as competition, as a very threat to her survival. She made it clear they were not to get in the way of her getting what she wanted. She continued to scream in their faces, hit them, scratch at them. It saddened us to see Annie and Ben so confused and disappointed, and at the same time, I felt an anger toward Emma that would well up inside me like a mother bear protecting her cubs. There was no way I was going to allow her to hurt my children. The initial disruption to the family was intense, but one we viewed as temporary. We had no idea then how wrong we were.

It was February 10, Emma's birthday, and she was turning two. We had a family party at home, just the five of us. Emma was puzzled as to what a birthday was all about. Because she didn't really understand any of it, the party ended up feeling a bit uneventful.

We met with the university clinic again for a follow-up visit. They were happy to hear that we had begun therapy with Emma to facilitate attachment and were pleased that Emma seemed to be physically thriving.

We began taking Emma to see the adoption therapist we had met with before. On most appointments, I would go with Emma alone. After several meetings, it was clear to the therapist that our daughter had not yet formed any kind of emotional attachment to anyone. We were assigned attachment work with her that would take anywhere from six months to a year to complete. We knew this would be hard work, but we honestly believed we were prepared and equipped for the job.

Our therapist began by putting us on a strict regimen. We funneled the meeting of all Emma's physical and emotional needs through just my husband and me. No one else was allowed to touch her, pick her up, or give her much attention. The goal was to demonstrate to her in a glaringly obvious way that we were her parents and we were going to meet her needs. We were told that our daughter was emotionally about five months old. She had likely suffered severe neglect, unsure of when she would get her next meal or be protected and safe, and unsure of who to look to in order to get those needs met. She was always on the lookout, constantly searching for who could be her "mom" for the day. And that could have been anyone: the checkout lady at the supermarket, a Sunday-school teacher, a grandmother, me, or anyone else she could charm into helping her. To her we were all the same.

We learned later that children with attachment issues use other people as objects to get what they want; they don't care about the relationship. It was about survival, and Emma would latch onto anyone who would help her survive. It was essential that she learn it was Andrew and me she could look to, that we were her parents and we would provide for her.

Since Emma was emotionally very infantile, we were counseled to try connecting with her in ways that parents typically do with infants. We encouraged her to make eye contact with us every thirty seconds to a minute. For nearly a year we rocked her, held her, bottle-fed her, sang to her, read to her, and snuggled with her. We met her demands on command, with little or no delay. She did not understand permanence, waiting, or cause and effect. It was exhausting work, work we were sure would yield good results.

Mealtimes were dreadful. Emma was obsessed with food, screaming for it. She often ate too quickly and vomited. Her anxiety was always high, but around food, it was at its highest. We went to spoon-feeding her pureed or finely chopped foods to help her slow down and wait between bites. We tried to teach her the concept of abundance, not scarcity. We wanted her to understand that the food wasn't going away, and nor was our protection, care, and love. There would always be enough for her.

We played all sorts of little games to teach her the concept of permanence. We played peek-a-boo. We tucked her bunny into bed, said, "We'll be back," and left the room. Minutes later we'd return to tell the bunny that we would always come back for him. We hid things and found them. We made all sorts of things disappear, and surprise! We'd find them again.

Emma didn't know how to hug. Every night we had hugging lessons. We tried to make it fun, and everyone got a turn. Annie and Ben ended up being her teachers. They modeled love and affection with us and tried their best to show her how to love.

The problem was, Emma didn't want our love. She didn't want hugs, snuggling, or affection, given or received. In fact, she didn't want anything to do with us at all. During hugging time, rocking, and snuggling, she tried to prove to us that she was not worth our time. She did her best to get us to reject her, to not love her, to leave her alone. She wanted to elicit a response she could predict, one that was familiar to her. She scratched at us, screamed, and tried to hurt herself. Until this time, the people Emma should have been able to trust had let her down. They hurt her. They rejected her. They left her alone. Those were the responses she knew well. She had learned that moms and dads weren't to be trusted. In fact, she considered us a threat to her survival too, because after all, she believed that those who took care of her would eventually neglect and hurt her as she had experienced many times before.

It was sad to see Emma trying so hard to sabotage what we wanted to give her. I felt angry with her foster family at times to the point where I couldn't let it go. I knew that obsessing over their neglect was not productive, even though it was a motivator for me to try harder, to invest more in helping Emma to heal. I wanted to do something about it. I wanted to be sure her foster family would never get another foster child. How could they have neglected to meet her needs when she was so helpless and dependent?

At the same time, it hurt to know that what we were trying to give to Emma, she would only reject. It felt personal, like she was rejecting *us*. Not just what we were trying to show her, teach her, or model for her, but

Andrew and I and Annie and Ben. The truth is, at the time Emma wasn't capable of receiving love from anyone. We were learning about attachment, but we didn't fully understand that then.

∞

On May 11, we had Emma dedicated at the church. Our niece Kristina was getting dedicated the same night, so it was a family affair. It seemed significant to dedicate Emma to the Lord that day, especially considering what we were learning about her each day. It was a reminder to us that Emma belonged to God, and He would guide us in helping her heal.

A month later, we received an e-mail telling us that the puppy we'd been waiting for was up for adoption. Almost a year earlier we'd decided to adopt a puppy for the kids. Annie and Ben loved animals and had been pleading with us to get a dog for quite some time. Ben and I are allergic to dogs, so we talked about it and decided on a poodle mix. We searched online and found a breeder out of Texas that sold Maltese-poodle mixes that were listed as "hypoallergenic." We fell in love with the pictures of Maltepoos, and we signed up to get one. Our name was put on a waiting list, and when we reached the top of the list, we had the opportunity to pick a puppy from new litters.

We explained to the kids that puppies are a big responsibility and cost money, so we bought a big Tupperware container that we labeled "puppy fund," which we filled with spare change and dollar bills. Grandparents and friends knew about the puppy fund, so the kids received rolls of quarters and bags of change for their birthdays and holidays that year. Ideally, we'd hoped to get our puppy in time to house-train before Emma arrived. No such luck. We waited almost a year—but we've always said our little Buddy was worth every day of waiting. By the year's end, we'd saved hundreds of dollars, and Buddy was flown up to Minnesota where we picked him up in his crate at the airport.

Annie and Ben were so excited to have the new puppy. Emma, being out of touch with so many things at the time, was initially unfazed and uninterested. The first morning after bringing Buddy home, the kids ran down to the kitchen to see him and let him out of his crate. Not more than two pounds at the time, he greeted Annie and Ben by jumping on them, wagging his tail, and licking their faces. "He still loves us! Look, Mommy, he still loves us today!" Ben exclaimed. Annie, too, said "Buddy loves us, Mommy, look at him! He's so happy to see us!"

I was thrilled to see Annie and Ben so happy, but I was a little puzzled by their statements. "Well, of course he still loves you, that's what puppies do best," I said, smiling. I sat on the floor with them and played with Buddy too, wondering what they were thinking.

It suddenly occurred to me why they were so genuinely surprised that Buddy's love for them hadn't changed overnight. With Emma, we'd waited with anticipation for her arrival. We'd talked endlessly about her, what she would be like, how much we couldn't wait to meet her, to adopt her. We'd looked at pictures, talked about names, prepared for her to be part of our family. Emma's coming, however, had turned out to be very different from what we'd expected or hoped. She came to us a fighter, a child who had fought for her very survival. Almost immediately after her arrival, Emma was clear in demonstrating to the kids that her purpose in coming was not for love. From their perspective, she didn't come to be loved or to give love. Emma had come to hurt. She didn't know how to love.

It saddened me to realize the connection they were making between Emma and Buddy, even though Buddy was a dog. Maybe Buddy had come at the right time after all. I suppose, after those first months with Emma, we all needed to feel loved back by someone we'd cared enough about to adopt into our family.

Interestingly, until having Buddy, I was not much of a dog lover. Growing up with dogs, I always viewed them as just that—dogs. They were nice to have around, but mostly they were just another responsibility. That all changed with Buddy. He instantly became my constant companion, my "baby." As dogs are so good at doing, Buddy just loves me as I am. In an extreme contrast to Emma, he's always ready for affection and love, and he freely gives it back. Whenever it seemed I was fighting off feelings of rejection from Emma, I'd hold Buddy. Just holding him for a moment somehow seemed to soften my heart.

CHAPTER SEVEN

Trauma

C ome on Emma, let's do lotion time!" It was almost time for Emma's nap. I set Annie and Ben up with something to do as I readied myself for our routine. At our last appointment, our therapist had recommended we add baby massage twice a day, before nap and bedtime, as a way of continuing to connect with Emma. Emma laid on the bed in her diaper as I began to rub lotion on her arms and legs.

"Arms, elbows, fingers," I said in a sing-song voice, Emma repeating after me. "Make it fun," our therapist had said. "Legs, knees, feet, toes!" we sang as we took turns squirting the lotion out.

For a few minutes Emma was okay. She played the game until I rubbed her back. Her arm flew out, then in, and she scratched herself on her stomach. We went back to arms and legs. I began to softly rub her head. As if automated, Emma's hand flew up and hit her head, over and over again.

"Emma? It's okay, Mommy's here. It's okay." Emma's eyes rolled back and she began to scream. Initially, I was able calm her down and she wanted to play again, but she drifted in and out of hysteria. Her head broke out into a sweat that soaked the sheets. She repeatedly scratched at and hit herself. When her eyes weren't rolled back, they looked vacant and empty. I swaddled her up and began to rock her like we'd done every day for months. She continued screaming, arching her back, and sweating until she collapsed into sleep.

What was that about? I was confused and concerned. This was a side of Emma I hadn't seen. As I sat in the rocking chair after she'd fallen asleep, I felt a little traumatized myself. I was mostly disturbed, not able to make sense of what had happened. I had no idea what to do to help her.

After talking to our therapist about it, we were encouraged to push Emma gently through these episodes so she could begin experiencing intimacy that didn't result in abuse or neglect. The whole process took one hour, ending with rocking Emma to sleep in emotional exhaustion. I felt a lot of anxiety going into baby massage, anxiety which I realized was not helpful to Emma. Still, our assignment was to push through it, so we did our best to continue on. Andrew tried to help by doing the bedtime routine whenever he could. It was exhausting for Emma and for us.

By now, Emma could no longer tolerate not being the center of attention. It didn't matter how much time and focus we directed toward her; she was a bottomless pit. We didn't understand at the time that kids like her are like empty buckets. We as adoptive parents try with great effort to fill up their buckets with love, security, and attention, not realizing their buckets are full of holes. Parents like us begin to feel depleted, and kids like Emma never get full.

Emma began to scream through meals and constantly get in trouble when the other kids were around. She spent a great deal of time in time-out, which we had her do in a Port-a-crib in the dining room. That way she'd never be too far away (remember, we were trying to facilitate her attachment)! She yelled and screamed through time-outs, figuring that if she had to be in another room, she could at least make sure we weren't having any fun without her.

We were shocked and disturbed, but mostly confused. Who was this little girl? What had happened to her? Were the therapies and what we were doing at home helping her? We were beginning to wear down. I was physically tired and emotionally exhausted all the time. After putting the kids to bed at night, Andrew and I would assess what seemed to be working and what wasn't, and we'd strategize for the next day. I spent hours researching attachment disorder online and devoured any books I could get my hands on to learn more.

Our family life was going rapidly downhill. So much of our time and energy was focused on Emma, and we all were paying a price. We were at a loss about what to do. I felt torn, working hard to do everything in my power to help Emma while trying to protect and comfort Annie and Ben. I wanted to show Emma love and teach her how to love, and I desperately wanted her to be able to receive and begin reciprocating that love. At the same time, it angered me that she didn't seem to care. She was working very hard to show us that she didn't want a relationship with any of us. And I hated the way she treated Annie and Ben. I'd have days when I felt like I didn't even like her, let alone love her. I'd feel horrible guilt over feeling resentment toward her. *What kind of terrible mother feels that way?* I'd ask myself. *Where did the thoughtful, caring mother I used to be go?* After all, Emma was not to blame for the neglect she had endured early on. I hurt for her and I ached inside, wanting to fix what had happened to her. That internal conflict seldom left me alone.

Our therapist was giving us an education about attachment and the brain. Rocking and movement was good for Emma, and because she was still so tiny, she fit into an infant's swing. We had one we'd used for Annie and Ben that was battery operated. I set it up in the kitchen so Emma could spend some time each day swinging nearby. One day I had her in the swing and was getting ready to make dinner. It had been an exhausting day, and the kids and I were all tired. The pre-dinner hour, or as I often referred to it, "the witching hour," was the time after naps, before Andrew was home for work. The kids were usually the most challenging during that time, and I was usually the shortest on patience.

I can't remember what it was Ben did, but he'd gotten into trouble, and I was going to give him a time-out in his bedroom. Normally very compliant, he surprised me by simply refusing to go. I ended up carrying him up the stairs to his bedroom with him screaming all the way. Once in his room, he kicked at his door and continued to scream and cry. I realized later that he, like all of us, had been experiencing the stress of our home life building and was due to blow a gasket.

Unfortunately, I was doing so poorly that day myself that Ben's time-out proved to be my breaking point. As if watching myself from a distance,

I walked into our bathroom and closed the door, locking it behind me. I was sobbing uncontrollably, unable to pull it together. I could hear Annie running upstairs calling, "Mommy?" And yet, I couldn't answer her. I couldn't do anything but sit there and cry. Soon Emma was screaming— her swing had stopped. Annie ran downstairs to start up the swing again, then ran up to tell Ben, who was also still screaming, that I couldn't hear him. She continued to do this, all the while calling for me.

It breaks my heart even today to think of how stressful and scary that afternoon must have been for her. It was a literal out-of-body experience for me, and one I'm not proud of. I somehow managed to call Andrew, although I could hardly speak. He was on his way to get his haircut on the way home from work, but hearing my voice, he came straight home instead. I didn't know it at the time, but he called my dad, who lived nearby, asking if he could come to the house and help me.

The two of them arrived almost at the same moment. I was still crying when they got there, barely able to explain what was happening. Looking back, I realize that the physical and emotional exhaustion and my anxiety and grief about our home life had taken its toll, and I had neglected to care for myself in the process. I also came to understand later that Emma's very presence in our home triggered my own feelings of rejection and isolation, which added to my sense of anxiety. For a short time after that, I was on a mild anti-anxiety medication that I could take as needed when I felt like I was going to lose control.

I understood that things at home were stressful, and it made sense why, but I couldn't figure out why I was so out of sorts. I wondered what on earth was happening to me. Why couldn't I just pull it together?

I believed at the time that if I would just work hard enough, things would eventually change. The truth is, looking back I don't know if I ever really believed to my core that I was doing enough to earn God's favor so that He would heal Emma. I thought I had to prove to Him that I was doing my part so that He would do what I was asking. My definition and understanding of grace was faulty and limited.

It was summer, and the days were long. At the start, Emma loved playing outside; it was her favorite place to be. She liked being pushed in a swing best. It was this summer, however, that we discovered Emma's unnatural fear of bugs. While she hadn't seemed to notice them before, she suddenly became obsessed with them. The very sight of a bug could send her over the edge. Similar to her reactions during baby massage, Emma would be in such a state of panic and fear that she would excessively sweat, scream, and sometimes check out in a way that we couldn't reach her, talk to her, or comfort her.

As we approached late summer, Emma spent more of her time inside due to her fear. It was a weekend, and Andrew was home. We were in the kitchen when we heard a loud thump in the living room, followed by a scream. Running into the room, the first thing I saw was blood. Emma was covered in it. It was on her face, dripping down onto her shirt and onto the floor. She was sitting on the floor next to our limestone coffee table.

Andrew swooped her up and hurried her into the kitchen. It was obvious that Emma had fallen onto the coffee table, bashing her head on the edge. I ran into the kitchen where Andrew was looking at Emma's head under the kitchen lights. She was screaming at this point, less from the pain and more in response to being held. She arched her back and thrashed around. She wanted down. Annie and Ben ran to get her stuffed bunny to give to her.

Her head was still bleeding badly, so together Andrew and I laid her down on the kitchen island so we could clean up her wound and bandage it up. Emma couldn't have been more than eighteen pounds then. And yet, for being so small, she was quite strong. It was all we could do to hold her down long enough to get her cleaned up. I tried comforting her with my words, which I learned was a mistake. Every time I spoke gently to Emma, she arched and screamed, her eyes rolling back, her face dripping with sweat. She couldn't tolerate our efforts to help her. It was as if she couldn't tolerate us being kind. I stopped speaking to her so as not to upset her any more than she already was. Andrew worked quickly, cleaning and bandaging her head. After what seemed like a long time, we finally got her cleaned up.

It was getting harder to know how to help Emma. Her outbursts were more frequent, and yet she seemed incapable of allowing us to help her, to comfort her. She didn't want us to touch her, hold her, or give her a hug, all the things we instinctively knew to do for children when they are distressed. We kept searching for ways to connect with her, and yet the harder we tried, the harder she worked to push us away. It was confusing too, because when we were around other adults, she'd seek their affection, especially if they were strangers.

I was still learning about the details of attachment disorder, and I was beginning to understand that intimate relationships are scary for kids like Emma, whereas strangers are safe. It is backward thinking and hard for us to initially understand. Kids like Emma are empty emotional vessels and are trying to fill up that empty place. Because they don't trust anyone and true, healthy intimacy is scary to them, they look outside of their intimate relationships to meet their emotional needs. What they don't understand is that what they are seeking can never fill the emptiness they have inside, because you can't find true intimacy with strangers. Even though strangers may have looked to Emma like they had her best interests in mind, it was a false intimacy.

Emma, like many unattached kids, was incapable of receiving our love and affection. She was stuck on the first tier of Maslow's hierarchy of needs, wondering still whether or not her basic needs, like food, shelter, and safety, would be met. Until she could successfully pass through that stage, she'd not be able to even grasp relationships and what they meant.

One night, I had dinner with some friends who asked about Emma— one of them a therapist. I shared with them our new discoveries and experiences, and my therapist friend said, "What you are describing sounds an awful lot like Post-Traumatic Stress Disorder." She went on to tell me that many of the symptoms Emma was displaying—sweating, screaming, dissociating, eye-rolling—were all common symptoms of PTSD. I left that night with a phone number for one of her colleagues, who specialized in working with trauma and brain-related issues.

I soon scheduled an appointment with my friend's colleague to get my first lesson in Post-Traumatic Stress Disorder. In that initial meeting, I learned a lot about trauma and the brain. I brought the therapist up to speed on Emma and what we'd been doing with her in therapy and at home for nearly a year. I described Emma's behavior and symptoms. I told her about baby massage. When I'd say, "I'm here, and I love you, Emma," she'd scream "No!" and check out again, screaming and scratching. She'd sometimes yell out Ma's name, her foster mother. When we tried to connect with her through play, Emma became hyper-aroused, wanting to please, but clearly in a state of panic and terror, unable to predict what was about to happen.

That hyper-aroused state was probably the way Emma looked before abuse, the therapist said, trying to be appeasing to prevent abuse, but inside filled with terror. The therapist believed that Emma was exhibiting clear signs of PTSD in response to some type of horrific event or events and/or ongoing physical or sexual abuse she had endured prior to coming to our home.

Thanks to that referral, we had some tangible interventions we could try right away. For starters, we could stop the things that were putting Emma into a trauma state, like baby massage. Putting Emma into a trauma state re-cemented old pathways in her brain that were not helpful. My friend's colleague works primarily with adults, so she referred us to a colleague named Cheryl, who specializes in working with children and trauma.

We were signed up the next month to attend a support group for parents of adopted children with attachment issues, offered by the agency that had done our home study in St. Paul. We left the kids with a sitter. When we arrived at the agency, we were surprised to see so many people there. There were about twenty-five chairs sitting in a circle, and nearly every seat was taken.

Emma's first-year therapist was facilitating the meeting. He led the meeting by reviewing some basic information about attachment, along with parenting strategies to facilitate bonding. Throughout the meeting, many of the parents shared personal stories about their experiences raising attachment-disordered children. Sitting there in the circle listening to everyone's stories was the first time Andrew and I realized we were not alone. As sad as it was to hear how discouraged many of the parents were feeling that day, it was relieving too. Until that meeting, we were the only people we knew who were raising a child with an attachment disorder. We'd begun to feel isolated and alone in the process.

Many of the stories and feelings shared in the group resonated with us. We spent some time after the meeting chatting with the couple sitting next to us. Another mom and I exchanged phone numbers before we left, and each of us encouraged the other to call on difficult days when we needed extra support and encouragement. It was comforting to know that someone out there understood exactly what we were going through.

A couple of other things happened over the summer that contributed to our stress. I ended up having a lumpectomy after discovering a lump in my breast that the doctors had difficulty identifying until it was removed. Andrew was laid off from work, which was difficult for him, having never experienced a lay-off before. These things temporarily added to our sense of feeling overwhelmed. Emma's adoption had been very expensive, and we had just put those payments behind us, but ongoing therapies, which we paid for out-of-pocket, cut into almost all of our savings. Our monthly budget had increased significantly. In the end, it was only a month that Andrew was out of work before he found a new job, but the stress during that time was great. We were finding it a great effort to surrender our worries and trust that we would be okay.

It was Andrew's birthday, and we were out to dinner with my parents, my brothers, and my sisters-in-law. It had been a while since we'd all been together, so we spent the first part of the evening getting caught up on everyone's news.

"How are things at home these days?" someone asked. It was our turn to share.

Everyone knew things had been challenging, but we hadn't yet really disclosed how difficult it had been of late and how much we were grieving. Andrew and I looked at each other, wondering if we should upset the party atmosphere.

Finally, one of us spoke. "We've been having a difficult time. To be honest, we are feeling overwhelmed and are struggling right now." I broke down, barely able to speak through the tears. Andrew was emotional too. We went on to explain what life had been like over the past months and the grief we were struggling with. We were grieving what we thought Emma would be, grieving the loss of our happy family. Our home life had gone from peaceful and fun to chaotic and stressed.

The truth was, our adoption of Emma so far had turned out to be very different than what we'd imagined, and admitting that was hard. We were grieving for Emma too, for what she'd endured and how she'd been hurt by those she should have been able to trust.

"How can we help?" the family asked. By the end of our night together, we'd decided on some scheduled prayer time together as a family. Soon after, we began meeting one night a month to pray together at our house.

The start of the school year was quickly approaching. Annie was getting ready to start first grade; Ben kindergarten. We were going to try Emma in preschool two afternoons a week so I could have some respite. Andrew had started his new job. He'd had a month at home and been able to help me out more with the kids. He had known how difficult my days were working with Emma, trying to balance meeting her needs while creating as much normalcy as possible for Annie and Ben. Being home for a whole month gave him the opportunity to see and experience firsthand how challenging that was to do.

By the end of the month, he insisted we find some help so that, when I wasn't focused on Emma, I'd have opportunities to spend some alone time with Annie and Ben. I was missing that, and they were too. Emma still viewed Annie and Ben as competition and continued to be abusive toward them, as well as sabotaging my time with them. I knew that spending some alone time with them would also help me to recharge. We realized that getting help would require a special person who would be willing to help us, someone who could understand our needs, especially Emma's, and be consistent with our parenting strategies. We began to pray, asking the Lord to help us find just the right person for our family.

"The agency needs to know about Emma," I said to Andrew one night after the kids had gone to bed. It was our usual nighttime routine of folding clothes in the living room. "What if another child has been placed with her foster family? Our therapists believe Emma was at the very least neglected, likely abused. I believe that too. If nothing else, I think the agency should know about that. The truth is, I'm so angry with Emma's foster parents, I just need to do *something*. If we can protect another child from being placed with them, I'll at least feel like what Emma went through was not totally in vain."

Andrew, reaching into the pile of clothes, looked pensive. I paused and watched him fold towels. Had he heard me? As I opened my mouth to ask him what he thought, he replied, "What did you have in mind? Do you want to write a letter?"

"No, I was thinking more along the lines of making a phone call."

"What would we say?"

"I want them to know what our therapists are saying about Emma, so that they'll look into her foster family. I want them to know that we don't hold them responsible, but with our information, something should be done."

"You've thought about this for a while, haven't you?" Andrew asked.

"I suppose I have. I'm so angry with Emma's foster family. Emma's paying an awful price for what they did to her, and we are too. I can't bear the fact that they might be fostering another child."

Over the course of the next year, two therapists submitted letters to the agency on our behalf, which included assessments of Emma's emotional state.

⌒

"How are things going with Emma?" the post-adoption social worker asked.

After we called our agency from Oregon, they decided to schedule a conference call with us to review our post-adoption information and get a more detailed update. Both our post-adoption social worker and the social worker in charge of the Thailand program were on the phone.

I was on the basement wall phone. Andrew sat next to me on the cordless phone. "Well, to be honest, it's been challenging," we told them. We went on to talk about how Emma was doing, the therapies we were involved in, and the progress we were seeing. We didn't want them to feel responsible, but at the same time, we wanted to be truthful with our report. The social worker responded with empathy, saying it sounded like things had been difficult and asking if we were getting other support from family and friends. She asked how things were between Emma and our other children. We told her that Emma's transition had so far been quite disruptive to Annie and Ben, and we'd pursued therapy for them too.

"You haven't finalized your adoption with Emma yet," she said. "Until you do, we are legally still her guardians. Do you think you still want to finalize Emma's adoption?"

The social worker went on to explain that had the agency been aware of Emma's issues, they never would have placed her with our family, because we had other small children in the home. And, she said, they knew how disruptive a child like Emma could be to a family like ours. Typically it's not a good match. "Do you feel like you've exhausted all of your resources?"

We were stunned that the agency was asking these questions. Of course we would still finalize, we said. "Adoption is permanent. Our intention was never to bring Emma home and then choose not to adopt her. She's our daughter. And no, we don't feel like we've exhausted *all* of our resources." We wondered how on earth, after just a year, anyone would have been able to answer yes to that.

We asked the post-adoption social worker if they had heard anything back from the Thailand branch in response to the letters our therapists had written. She answered, "We looked through our paperwork, and the other families that adopted children coming out of that foster home have had no complaints."

That was it. It was clear by her tone that we were not appreciated for having sent the letters. We said, "So, because other families haven't contacted you since placement with complaints, what you're saying is that it's not possible this foster family was ever neglectful or abusive to their foster children?"

That didn't make any sense to us. "What about our therapist's assessments of Emma?" we asked. And the International Adoption Clinic, what about their assessment? We couldn't believe our ears. At the time, three different specialists had assessed Emma, and all had concluded that she had severe attachment issues. One had diagnosed her as having severe post-traumatic stress.

That's when the phone call went rapidly downhill. "Listen," the social worker said. "I am very schooled in the field of attachment, and I'm telling you, all of us have attachment issues of some sort." Her voice began to take on a sharp, edgy tone, getting louder as she spoke. "Besides, I don't even know if I'd trust some therapist who calls himself an 'attachment specialist' anyway. Attachment therapies can be very controversial."

We sat in stunned silence, looking at each other as we held our phones to our ears. I can never think of what to say on the spot when I'm flustered. I was mute, trying to absorb everything I was hearing.

Andrew said, "We can assure you we are not involved in extreme controversial therapies with Emma. We know about those too. Our therapists are practical and grounded, and we trust their expertise. You may not trust what our therapists have to say, but what about us? You can challenge our therapists, but now you are beginning to challenge our experience."

I don't even remember what was said next. I remember hearing her answer back, her voice defensive and angry, almost yelling. I heard Andrew trying to say something, but I couldn't hear a thing he said over her voice. She talked over him, not allowing him to speak.

The next thing I heard was Andrew saying, "We are going to hang up the phone. We are not willing to continue this conversation with you as long as you are yelling at us. We'd be open to talking to you again when we can have a respectful conversation. Good-bye." I was impressed by how calm Andrew was, even to the end when he couldn't get a word in. He motioned for me to hang up.

We sat there for what seemed like a long time. We were in shock over what had taken place. It was bizarre, really. We couldn't figure it out. Wasn't the social worker supposed to be reassuring, supportive, and professional? We wondered if the agency was concerned that we would hold them liable for Emma's attachment issues, but we didn't know. I took offense to her telling us she was "very schooled in attachment issues." Like many unique, challenging situations, being "schooled" through education is not the same as being "schooled" through experience. I sensed from our conversation that this social worker didn't have the first idea of what living with a child with severe attachment issues was really like.

I was sure the worker in charge of the Thailand program would call the next day to apologize or debrief. After introducing us to the post-adoption social worker on the phone, she'd been quiet throughout the rest of the conversation. Unfortunately, we never heard from the agency again. I considered calling back weeks later, but frankly, I was hurt by the conversation we'd had and didn't have the energy to go through another one like it. It seemed like once the agency heard we'd be moving ahead to finalize, they no longer were concerned. Their responsibility as Emma's guardians would be over, and they were done with us.

School started for the kids, and we welcomed the routine. Preschool for Emma didn't start until the next month. In the meantime, we met with Emma's teachers to prep them on some of her issues and how to respond best to her needs. Being a small school, they didn't have special-needs services like a district school, but they were very willing to offer Emma a place there. They knew our family from having had Annie and Ben in the previous years. I was looking forward to having a couple of hours to myself those two afternoons a week to run errands, meet a friend for coffee, or just have time at home alone.

CHAPTER EIGHT

Sweat and Tears

We began work with Cheryl in October, almost one year after Emma's homecoming. We worked intensely with her over the course of the next two years. She did an amazing job with Emma and worked hard to help us restore some balance in our family. Emma saw her twice a week. For six months of that time, Annie and Ben met with her too. We wanted them to have a place outside of home where they felt supported. She helped Annie and Ben understand Emma's issues in a way that made sense to them. Cheryl also became my advocate and supporter, helping me deal with the complexities that come with parenting a child like Emma. She was my permission slip to sanity. Talking with her helped me to normalize our seemingly abnormal reality. She gave me assignments that were about taking care of me, and she held me accountable to doing them. Many times I showed up to her office in tears, overwhelmed and feeling defeated. On those days, she was my therapist before meeting with Emma. Most of the time I felt like a crazy person, and I continually beat myself up for not being able to love Emma more, give her more, in a sense "fix" her. Cheryl helped me to understand that it wasn't my job to fix Emma, and what was more, that Emma might not be "fixable."

After weeks of my showing up in the same emotional state, she asked me, "When are you going to stop?"

"Stop what?" I asked.

"When are you going to stop beating yourself up for what happened to Emma? You act responsible for everything that happened to her before she came."

I hadn't thought of it like that before, but she was right. It wasn't rational, but I *did* feel and behave as though I was responsible for what had happened to Emma. Logically I knew I wasn't, but as Emma's mom, instinctively I believed it was my job to protect her, and before she came she hadn't been protected and safe. It took me some time until I was able to stop behaving the way I was, and much longer for me to emotionally internalize what our therapist was repeatedly saying to me.

Cheryl did a lot of work with Emma in regards to dealing with trauma. With her help, we saw Emma make progress in tackling irrational fears, getting in touch with her body, decreasing self-harm, and handling anxiety. She knew Emma well and could recognize subtle signals that few others would see. Emma's face, for example, would change when she was operating out of a trauma state of mind. One side of her face would droop, making her eyelid sag. Her eyes would have a vacant look about them, one that seemed to look past you instead of at you. We could see Emma's face change from day to day, sometimes moment by moment, depending on how she was doing. It reached a point where just by looking at Emma at the start of therapy, Cheryl could say, "So, Emma's in a good place today," or "It looks like we've got some trauma work to do." She called it correctly every time. We learned to recognize that look and adjust our interactions with Emma accordingly at home, just like in therapy.

Cheryl was very supportive of enrolling Emma in preschool. She felt school would give us an idea of where Emma was emotionally—if she was beginning to trust that her needs were going to be met.

Emma's first day finally came. She was excited about going, and I was excited for her to go. The first couple of days seemed to go without incident. She was wound up and in a bit of a manic state when I picked her up from school, a good indication that she was tired. Cheryl suggested I put her down for some quiet time when she got home to wind down.

A couple of weeks into preschool, I opened Emma's door to let her know that her quiet time was over. I knew she had been awake for a while, having listened to her talking to her bunny for the past few minutes. She startled when I opened the door, sat up, jumped down from her bed, and sped past me out of the room. As usual, I surveyed the room. She was in the habit of picking the paint off her walls, one small chip at a time. She was meticulous about it, her small fingers picking each chip off, each piece no bigger than a ladybug. At times there would be paint chips all over the bed and floor; other times she would drop the chips down her heating vent. We had tried in vain to get her to stop. She would start by picking just a little, her obsessive-compulsive tendencies would kick in, and she couldn't stop.

Today there was no paint to be found. One glance at her sheets, however, and I knew something didn't look right. I bent down to take a closer look. I saw hair. Black strands of hair covered the bed and floor. I called Emma back into the room.

"What is this?" I asked.

"My hair," she said.

"How did your hair get there?" I said. I knew the answer, but I wondered what she would say.

"I put it there. From here," she said, pointing to the top of her head. We'd done work in therapy around issues of self-harm.

"Honey, when you pull your hair out, that hurts your body. It's your job to take care of and protect Emma's body."

Emma's hair-pulling got worse. In addition, she'd have days on the weekends when she didn't want to come out of her room. She was miserable being there, and yet she refused to come out. By the end of the fourth week of school, we got a phone call from her teacher. I had a sinking feeling when I answered the phone. She asked how Emma was doing. I told her that Emma seemed to be growing increasingly stressed as the weeks passed. I mentioned her hair-pulling and asked what they were observing at school.

She went on to say that Emma was having a difficult time with transitions. She was unable to sit still during singing or sharing time, obsessing over things in the room. This was not a surprise, as she did this regularly with things at home. She'd focus on something and get stuck, unable to let go or move on. She'd repeat words over and over again until she was firmly redirected. It was clear this was happening at school too.

Emma's teacher told me that her behaviors were disruptive to the point where extra help was needed for her during structured activities. Emma was unable to follow simple directives. Her anxiety was high because being among so many other children put her in a place of panic, and she worried she was not going to get her needs met.

Like Cheryl had predicted, school was challenging Emma's beliefs about what we were trying to teach her. We realized she wasn't yet ready to be put into an environment that set her back in believing she was safe and would be taken care of. Had she been at our district school it might have been okay, because she could have been assigned a paraprofessional to give her one-on-one help. But at our neighborhood preschool, they were not equipped for kids with special needs. We'd known that going in, but thought we'd try it anyway.

The director of the program asked to meet with us. Andrew went to the meeting with me. In a nutshell, the director explained they were simply not able to handle Emma's special needs at school. We understood, but we were sad to pull Emma out. It would be another year before we'd try school again. I was discouraged and disappointed. Not only would I not be getting predictable breaks, but the event was also a reminder of how much further we had to go in helping Emma.

Around that time we got a call from the adoption agency in Minnesota that had done our home study. Would we come and speak to a group of prospective adoptive parents and share our adoption story? I honestly thought they were joking. So far, our story hadn't been a gleaming picture of a warm, fuzzy adoption. The agency knew that. They'd done follow-up visits after placement and had been very supportive and helpful in referring us to valuable resources. In fact, they'd been the ones who initially put us in contact with the International Adoption Clinic at the university and with Emma's first therapist.

"Are you sure you want us to speak to your prospective parents? You know our story has been challenging from the beginning."

"Absolutely," our social worker responded. "Your kind of story is just as important if not more so to people considering adoption, because it includes the realities of adoption many don't consider."

It was refreshing to feel like they got it. They understood and didn't treat us like we were the only adoptive parents who had ventured down the road we were on. We agreed to speak at their next meeting.

Andrew and I went together with Emma to the meeting a few weeks later. We stood in front of the room and told our story. We tried to describe our life after adoption as truthfully and accurately as possible. If I remember correctly, there were just a few couples there that day. They stared back at us with little expression and a look that I recognized as having been my own in the past. It was a look that said, "That's sad for you, and we feel bad. However, our adoption story will be different. That kind of thing won't happen to us, and if it does, we'll be fine because we're prepared."

They were interested in seeing Emma. She was her typical self with strangers, irresistibly charming and sweet. She loved being the focus of attention, and she soaked it up. The sight of her was enough to make just about anyone who ran into Emma think to themselves, "How could that cute little thing have that many emotional problems? It can't be *that* bad."

That, sadly, was the reaction we received over time from some friends too, those we had trusted and thought we could count on. Though there were many who stood beside us, supporting us and praying for us, others simply didn't believe us. Over time, we heard things that were said about us, and some of it was hurtful. Friends of ours, people whom we'd once considered close, told others they thought we were making a big deal over nothing. They said Annie and Ben had been easy children. Emma was normal but our first challenging child, and we just didn't know how to handle her.

More than Emma's behaviors, more than the stress that seemed to overtake our family, the hurt of not being believed sometimes felt the worst. I felt like I was hanging on by a thread most of the time, and we were living in chaos every day. To have that discounted, minimized, or simply rejected as truth was on some days too much to bear. I fluctuated between anger and sadness over it.

On one hand, we understood how people could come to the conclusion that Emma was normal. Kids with attachment disorders act phony around others, especially strangers whom they think they can control with manipulation. Emma was incredibly charming with strangers, always engaging them in conversation while acting cute and bubbly. People gushed over her, saying things like, "What a cutie! She's a doll. She is absolutely darling!" Annie and Ben were often unintentionally ignored because they were quiet. It was hard on all of us, because we knew what Emma was like when we were alone.

Nearly all parents of children with attachment disorders deal with this reality on some level. It was amazing how Emma could turn on the act like a light, in an instant, and turn it off just as quickly. It fed the growing resentment we all felt toward her. And it fed the horrible feeling of being misunderstood and judged by others, which perpetuated feelings of isolation. That reality is something we live with to this day. There are still many who do not understand, and we don't expect them to. They look at us from the outside and make their own judgments about what has happened. That's just the way it is. While the attitudes are not voiced aloud to us, we know they're there. I used to feel like we had to explain our story to everyone so they would understand. With the help of therapy, I learned that wasn't true.

As the years passed, I reached a point where I no longer invested in maintaining close friendships with people who were not willing to acknowledge Emma's problems or believe our story. Emma had obviously become such a dominant part of our lives that to not be able to talk about her honestly shifted once-close friendships to a shallow and awkward state. My time away from Emma was precious, and I struggled as it was to stay invested in friendships that had more depth and substance.

At the same time, there were friends and even acquaintances who demonstrated the depth of their caring for us in sometimes surprising ways. There were times when God knew I needed a tangible act of mercy. I'd get an e-mail or card in the mail; a phone call would come in; someone would stop by or drop off a meal. Friends continued to pray for us and for Emma. That was the greatest gift of all.

We'd been so inwardly focused on our family since Emma arrived that we quickly became out of touch socially. We didn't see our friends anymore because we were still intensely working with Emma to attach, and it was recommended that I not do playgroups with Emma that first whole year. We were also told not to put Emma in any kind of nursery or childcare situation without us present. Looking back, I believe that was unhealthy for us, but at the time we were doing anything and everything professionals recommended we do. We naturally began to feel isolated and disconnected from the outer world. I grieved the loss of seeing my friends over and over again. Losing the support of others added to our grief.

Our first prayer meeting with my extended family took place that fall. Our meetings, which turned out to be held once a month, consisted of sharing prayer requests and spending time in prayer together as a group. For the next year, those prayer meetings helped sustain us, encouraging us to remain hopeful and optimistic. Coincidentally, my mom battled breast cancer that year as well. Talking about Emma, Mom's cancer, and other requests allowed our family to bond in a new way.

At the end of the first meeting, Andrew and I happened to mention that we were putting thought into hiring some part-time help, and we asked for prayer that the Lord would lead us to the right person for our family.

After everyone left, Andrew and I debriefed. It was good to have some time to really talk about things. The night had turned out to be just what we needed. We felt cared for, and we knew my family would continue to be faithful in praying for us. Releasing what was on our hearts allowed us to be clearheaded, and we began strategizing with a new sense of energy.

With Emma no longer in school, we got serious about finding a part-time nanny to help us out. Ideally, we decided it would be best if we could find someone to live with us. Our basement was largely unused. We decided to convert it into an apartment and look for someone who could live in it and provide part-time help. Our basement project began that weekend. We typed out and printed an ad for a part-time, live-in nanny that we posted to a local Christian college the next day. We couldn't imagine at the time who it might be, but we trusted the Lord would provide. I went to bed feeling more hopeful than I'd felt in a while.

The next day I got a phone call from my sister-in-law, Lisa. She told me she had some interesting news. The night before, when she and my brother Dave were at our house to pray, they'd hired Lisa's cousin Soni to babysit their girls. When they returned home, Soni stayed a while to talk. She had asked Dave and Lisa about their evening out. Without mentioning details, they shared the basics of our situation and why we were getting together to pray.

"I got an e-mail from Soni today," Lisa said. "I'd like to pass it on to you. We never told Soni you were looking for help. We shared with her only general information about your adoption story with Emma. Soni's a senior at Bethel College right now and a psychology major." After we hung up, Lisa sent a copy of Soni's e-mail.

Lisa & Dave,

Thank you for sharing with me just some of the things concerning Emma. Ever since the day I heard about Kristi and Andrew adopting her, I've been praying for her. God just has laid her on my heart, and even though I've never met her, there is a special place for her in my heart. Right now, I don't know what or if there is anything I can do to help, but I'm praying about it so much. I woke up this morning just thinking about Emma and praying for her and just asking God if there is something more He wants me to do. I would love to talk to you both more and see what doors God opens. Isn't it amazing—the connections that aren't always so clear and don't always make sense right away, but God has for his children. Before I even came to your house last night I had been praying that afternoon about different desires and passions God has laid on my heart. In short, I asked that God would channel them and guide them to where He can use me. So, I'm not sure how or if there is a place for me in Emma's life right now or a year from now, or maybe she will just always be in my prayers...but God knows, and I will continue to seek Him

and pray for my beautiful little sister in Christ! It's exciting.
Because of Him,
Soni

Soni turned out to be an answer to prayer and a great fit for our family. While waiting on her decision to come live with us, she happened to find, of all things, my dad's Bible lying on the side of the road while she was driving in her car. What were the chances, she said, that she'd find a Bible on the side of the road with my dad's name on it just while she'd been praying for a sign about the job we'd offered her?

After calling my brother Dave to find out if the name on the Bible was any relation to him, she was convinced. We found out later that my dad had mistakenly driven off with his Bible on top of his car. It had fallen to the side of the road somewhere near their home. What seemed strangely coincidental, we believed to be the hand of God. Soni did a wonderful job with the kids, and we quickly grew to love her like family.

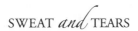

The living room was all too quiet. Anyone with small children knows that if a child is in a room and the only sound you hear is silence, it's time to get in there and see what's going on. I had experienced it many times before with Annie and Ben, finding them up to their ears in typical childhood mischief. I had come upon Annie at the age of three, in our bathroom during her nap time, covered in lotion, wearing a pair of my heels, and standing on our scale wearing only a diaper. I'd discovered Ben about to bite into a handful of lit Christmas lights. I wasn't sure what I would find now as I peeked around the corner, but I was certain I would find Emma in a similar kind of situation.

I tiptoed down the hall to the living room. Buddy, now ten pounds and fully grown, had been napping on the sofa. When I looked into the room, Emma was kneeling beside him. She had her hands clutched around Buddy's neck. She was holding his head up and squeezing his throat.

Her wide-open eyes stared directly into his. Her lower lip was jutted out, and her arms and head were trembling. He looked like he'd just opened his eyes. It looked as though she was attempting to choke him, squeezing with all her might.

"Emma!" I said in a short, loud voice. Her whole body jumped when she heard me speak. Like a light that had been switched on, she instantly transformed her face. With a sweet and loving smile she looked at me and said, "Look, Mommy, I'm petting Buddy." She began gently stroking his back with her hand.

I shook my head. *What was that? Did what I just see really happen?*

I wondered over the next couple of days if it had been an isolated incident. I wasn't going to risk something happening to Buddy again, so I began to make sure Emma was never alone with the dog. I hid out of her sight if I saw her going into a room alone where Buddy was sleeping and watched her without her knowing I was there. Each time, she would look over her shoulder to see if anyone was watching her. Then, silently, she would approach him. She continued to do what she had done on that first day I caught her. She'd grab him by the throat and literally try to wring his neck. Each time I announced my presence, she would practically jump out of her skin.

The look on Emma's face was what disturbed me the most. In an instant she could change from looking almost devilish to looking angelic. And she immediately, on the spot, had a story about what she was doing. Usually she said she was petting Buddy.

This continued for the next several years, and we were vigilant about making sure Emma was never alone with the dog, or with any small animal, for that matter. We learned soon after that this rule applied to babies and small children too. Anyone Emma viewed as smaller, weaker, or more vulnerable, she would try to harm if she thought no one was watching.

It really disturbed me to think that Emma had it in her to harm something or someone in that way. I guess we all have that in us, but she was able to act on it without a care or thought—least of all regret. It saddened me too, and I constantly wondered, what happened to her? What has she endured, seen, or experienced already in her short life?

Christmas was bittersweet that year. Andrew's parents were in town.

There were a lot of emotional triggers for Emma. She reacted to the decorations, the tree, the change in the weather, the change in the dynamics of the house with my in-laws around. Cheryl suggested that this was Emma's first Christmas being aware, not checked out like she'd been the year before. Christmas had come at a time not long after Emma's arrival. The confusion and fear she wasn't capable of experiencing the first year reared its head a year later. Her anxious and acting-out behaviors were at a fever pitch. Andrew and I grieved through the holiday, feeling loss again for ourselves and for Emma, and sadness over the state of our family.

CHAPTER NINE

Fries, Dip, and Pills

Food continued to be a big issue for Emma. We did everything we could think of to reassure her that she was going to get food at mealtimes. As I began to prepare meals, I'd set her plate, fork, spoon, and cup at her place at the table as a reminder that she had a place and would get to eat. She'd hover in the kitchen, almost pacing, always wanting to know what we were having, when we'd be eating. I'd say to her, "This is what we're having for dinner. We'll be eating in a few minutes, and there will be enough food."

It was a test of her patience and trust. She was learning to wait, and we were teaching her to trust us that we would follow through. We'd been doing it since the day she came home, and yet, instead of the task getting easier, her anxieties about food were only growing worse. When we'd finally sit down to eat lunch, for instance, instead of experiencing relief over getting her food, she'd immediately ask, "What are we having for dinner?" It was frustrating. She'd just spent the last hour obsessing about what we were having for lunch. Before her first bite, even, she wanted to know what we were having for dinner?

That type of behavior became very typical for her. She was never able to be in the moment, but always wondering what was next. Each time we arrived at that next thing, it was "what's next" all over again. Restaurants were horribly stressful for Emma. Not being able to see the food being prepared was too much for her. She couldn't trust that food would ever come. Waiting would put her in a trauma state, crying and sweating by the time food arrived despite having a snack or bread while we waited. And yet we continued to eat out once in a while, in hopes that she would later be able to experience restaurants without incident.

One particular Friday night in March, we took the kids to a fun hamburger and malt shop. It was a new restaurant in a restored auto mechanics garage, and we had wanted to try it out. Annie and Ben loved it. There were games to play at the table, and the host told them that hidden somewhere in the restaurant was a Mr. Potato Head. If they found it, they'd get a prize.

The fun was soon dampened, however, by Emma's anxiety. The toys were not enough to keep her occupied. I had forgotten to bring a snack for her, and I was paying the price. Her head was wet with sweat, and she was crying, saying "Fries and dip, fries and dip," a line she typically repeated while waiting for food. Fries and ketchup were her favorite food. We think the taste of fries and chips symbolized safety and comfort for her. Whenever her social worker would come for her monthly visits in Thailand, she would bring Emma a bag of chips. We're guessing that Emma's foster mother and father were kind to her before those visits, making sure she was bathed and fed, and it's unlikely they abused her in the days before the social worker came. Emma was nonverbal, so they didn't have to worry about her saying anything. In fact, it's likely Emma got whatever she wanted on the days of those visits, because the social worker's notes indicated that Emma seemed spoiled, throwing tantrums when she didn't get her way. The paperwork said that her foster mother always gave in to Emma during their scheduled meetings. Those visits represented safety for Emma, and she associated that feeling with the taste of fried potatoes. She obsessed about all food, but fries were the pinnacle of her dining experience.

Andrew and I were both short on patience that night. We'd been out to eat so many times before, and that night it felt like our patience was fast disappearing. When was Emma going to get it? Nothing we said could reassure her. She was so out-of-sorts that our fun night out was quickly turning into a disaster. Annie and Ben were no longer having fun, and they sat in their chairs in silence. Andrew and I didn't say much either as we tried to redirect Emma's attention away from her obsession with fries.

By the time our food came, we ate in silence, each of us looking down at our plates. Andrew tried to keep the conversation going, but nobody felt much like talking anymore. I was in tears by the time we left the restaurant. We didn't know at the time that the next four years of family outings would yield similar outcomes, which I guess is the gift of not being able to see into the future.

I was still feeling down about our outing by the time we arrived at our next therapy session just days later. "This obsession with fries is driving me crazy!" I said. "Sometimes I wish I could feed Emma fries until she can't stand them anymore, even if it makes her sick!" I felt relieved to get that off my chest. I could always count on Cheryl to listen to me without judgment and not to react in horror to anything I said.

"Why don't you?" she replied. I looked at her in disbelief. "What?" I said. "What are you talking about?"

She looked back at me and calmly said, "Why don't you feed her fries until she doesn't want any more? She just might realize that fries can't provide her with the emotional comfort she really wants. No, it's not the healthiest thing in the world, but she's not going to die on a fry diet. You could temporarily supplement her nutrition with a children's vitamin. If you want to try it, I support you."

It hadn't occurred to me that what I was saying just minutes ago could really happen. I thought about it for a moment. It would be interesting to see how long Emma could go on just fries, and if she could make the connection toward understanding that fries couldn't really comfort her in the way she needed. "Okay," I finally said, "let's do it."

I told Andrew about my meeting with Cheryl. He was behind the experiment, so we began the "fry diet" immediately. We stocked up on huge bags of frozen French fries from the grocery store. The first day Emma came into the kitchen for breakfast, acting nonchalant, I handed her a plateful of fries and a small bowl of ketchup. You'd think I had handed her the moon. Her eyes lit up as she let out a literal shriek of delight. She happily dipped away at those fries, smiling throughout the whole meal. She was perfectly giddy, like she'd won a prize. Lunchtime came, and the scene was the same. After nap, more fries. Then dinner, fries again.

This went on for days. As our therapist had recommended, we supplemented her diet with a children's multivitamin each day.

We stayed up-to-date on the diet during our weekly therapy sessions. Andrew and I let Emma know that at any time, she could choose to have something else to eat. Surely, I thought, she will tire of eating fries, and we will have cured her of her fry obsession. Like many times before, I'd underestimated Emma's staying power. Fifty-seven meals and nineteen snacks later, Emma made the decision that she was done, for now, with fries. When I handed her that last steaming hot plate, she looked up at me and said, "Emma's sad." Then she did something else she'd never done before: she let me hug her, and she hugged me back. I couldn't believe it. Was it a coincidence, or was it possible, like Cheryl had said, that Emma made a connection between fries and emotional comfort? I couldn't wait to ask Cheryl what she thought at our next meeting. She told me it was hard to know for sure, but it was definitely possible that some connection had been made.

I wish I could say that Emma's obsession with fries ended that day. Unfortunately, that's not the case. French fries continued to be one of her favorite foods, and food remained a source of anxiety for her, although the intensity of her stress went down enough over time that she was able to eat in restaurants without the wait sending her into a trauma episode.

Emma's disturbing behaviors continued to escalate over the next few months. She sweated excessively and screamed out during sleep. She thrashed around and ground her teeth. She'd bite the face of her favorite toy bunny, screaming a horrific scream while doing it. She eventually chewed the face right off and ripped the insides out. She picked at her fingernails and toenails until they bled. She continued to peel the paint off her walls and rip apart her books. The hair on her head was getting thinner by the day, as a result of her hair-pulling episodes. Anything we left her alone with, she destroyed. Soon, her room looked like a cell: a mattress on the floor with a dresser turned to face the wall.

At times it was all I could do not to pull out my own hair trying to figure Emma out. Thinking about it was not time well spent, since none of her behaviors made rational sense. I was doing my best to understand her, all the while disturbed to my core by the things I saw her do.

By midsummer, her self-harming behaviors grew worse. They were inhibiting our ability to work with her at home and in therapy. Cheryl and I talked about the possibility of getting Emma on some type of anti-anxiety medication for a while so that we could work intensely on giving her tools and other outlets for anxiety. Emma was operating out of a "trauma place" most of the time in those days, so it was essential that we help her gain the tools that would enable her to operate out of a new place, a safe place that she could predict. The plan was that once we'd achieved that, we'd wean her off the medication.

After I shared with Andrew my discussion with Cheryl, we decided to pursue medication for Emma. Andrew agreed that it could only be helpful. He'd seen Emma's self-destructive behaviors and was worried, too, that therapy was becoming less and less effective due to her high level of anxiety. We didn't know a thing about psychiatry. Where would we begin? How would we find the right children's psychiatrist for Emma? We began to pray about it and ask the Lord to lead us to the right person. In the meantime, Cheryl was working on having a referral for us at our next meeting.

We didn't have to wait long. The next weekend, my mom went to a high school reunion. There she ran into an old classmate who, interestingly enough, was a pediatric psychiatrist at the University of Minnesota. Mom and Dad ended up sharing our story with this gentleman that night. By the end of their conversation, he'd given Mom his contact information and told her to tell us to give him a call. The amazing thing was, we hadn't told my parents yet that we were seeking out a psychiatrist. When they called us with this doctor's information, we were surprised at the coincidence. Again, we believed it was not a coincidence, but another answer to prayer and a reminder that God knows what we need even before we do.

We scheduled an appointment for the second week of August for Emma's psychiatric evaluation and gathered as much of the paperwork we had on Emma as we could. We had her medical records, her therapy assessments, her therapy notes, and her paperwork from Thailand. As prepared as possible, Andrew, Emma, and I made our way to the clinic.

Andrew and I were nervous about the meeting, not knowing what to expect. The outcome we hoped for was a prescription for medication, but it was important to us that the doctor understand the efforts we'd been putting forth. We wanted him to know that medication wasn't our first attempt at helping Emma.

The doctor came out to the waiting room to bring us back to the room himself. He was friendly and personable. Emma flashed him her award-winning smile before we followed him down the hallway to our meeting room. We sat and told him our story, bringing him up to speed on therapies and our daily life at home. We handed him our paperwork and a picture I'd taken of Emma sleeping. At that time she was sweating excessively during sleep, soaking her sheets with her head. One night when we peeked in on the kids, I moved her from the wet spot under her head and took a picture. Her hair was wet and stringy, and the wet spot on her sheet was the size of a large dinner plate. The doctor observed Emma while we talked, all the while actively listening to us.

It didn't take him long to diagnose Emma as having Generalized Anxiety Disorder. He also confirmed Emma's other diagnoses, saying they sounded consistent with what we'd described. He asked if we'd consider medication to help lower her anxiety. We were relieved as we told him we were open to adding medication on top of her therapies and were hopeful that the combination would enhance her progress.

By the time our meeting was over, we had a prescription for an anti-anxiety drug we could give Emma as needed. The doctor did a wonderful job of educating us on anti-anxiety meds and what they can do, as well as talking to us about dosages and administration.

We were pleased with how the meeting had gone and were thankful again for another connection made with someone who had proved to be helpful. We started Emma on medication right away. After several weeks, it became obvious that the medication was having little to no effect. After discussing it with our doctor, we ended up with a different medication that seemed to help take the edge off. Unlike the first one, which could be given as needed, the new drug had to build up in Emma's system before we'd begin to see any change.

I have to admit, we were too optimistic about what medication could do for Emma. It sounds ridiculous now, but at the time, I think we thought medication would transform our daughter into a calm, loving little being. Our desperation to have Emma "get better" clouded our view of reality. Medication didn't change her personality, but in the end, it lowered her anxiety enough that she was able to make some progress in her therapies and at home. Her self-harming behaviors didn't subside altogether, but they did decrease, enough that she was able to learn other ways to work out her anxieties that weren't harmful to herself or others.

While we worked on these things in therapy, finding hair in Emma's room had become a routine experience. We were worried about her and wondered what else she was doing during her nap time and other times in her room alone. Cheryl and I discussed installing a video monitor in Emma's bedroom so we could see for ourselves what she'd been up to. We purchased a video monitoring system, and Andrew installed it right away, setting it up so the camera in Emma's room would record her during nap time. I could watch simultaneously downstairs on our television or watch it later on tape. Andrew happened to be home the next day, so we decided to watch Emma together during her nap.

We learned over the next few weeks that along with pulling her hair, Emma continued to pick at her skin, peel paint, tear books or pieces of paper, and rip her sheets. The most interesting of her behaviors was one we hadn't seen before. She spent anywhere from thirty minutes to an hour covering herself with saliva by putting her fingers in her mouth. It was clearly her way of self-soothing, and the last thing she did before falling asleep.

With Emma being just three years old, she still desperately needed naps. If we had days when we weren't home to nap her, we paid a high price later. She was easily overstimulated by late afternoon and completely wired all evening, despite her early bedtime at seven o'clock. Her negative behaviors were doubly intense when she was tired, so we made it a priority to nap her whenever possible.

It was fall again, one year into our meetings with Cheryl, and we decided it would be a good idea for Emma to receive an occupational therapy assessment in addition to psychological therapy. Cheryl thought it would be a good idea since Emma was displaying a number of sensory issues. We had her evaluated, and it was determined that OT would be good for her. She was severely delayed developmentally in several ways. Her core balance was poor, she had a variety of sensory issues, and she displayed poor motor planning. She was out of touch with her body, not knowing where it began and ended. Her language development was also severely delayed, and it was determined that she would benefit from speech therapy too. We began taking Emma to receive occupational therapy in St. Paul.

The news of Emma's disabilities was discouraging because they were so inconsistent with the paperwork we'd received on Emma from Thailand. It turned out that what had been written about Emma's development was almost entirely a work of fiction. The reports had said that Emma loved to sing songs, ride a bike, play games. The occupational therapists we were working with said that Emma clearly did not have the abilities to do any of those things, as she was too far behind in several basic areas of development. We could see it too, from living with her, and it was validating to have the occupational therapists observe what we'd experienced.

My anger flared up again at Emma's foster family. Clearly, they had been through fostering children before and knew what to say about where Emma should be in her progress at certain times. Almost all of what they'd reported was a lie. It was difficult to feel so angry and so helpless to do anything about it at the same time. I talked with Cheryl about it several times. Just voicing my thoughts was somewhat helpful, and she was able to validate my feelings of anger and ongoing frustration.

Through all of this, I have learned more about God's grace. I wanted justice, not grace, for Emma's foster family. What they did was wrong. In no way was it fair. I was humbled and troubled as I thought about these things. The truth is, God is not fair. And thank goodness He's not. If He were fair, my sinful nature would send me straight to hell with no detours or pit stops along the way. Jesus came for me as much as He came for them—for Emma's foster family and others like them. Grace, while free and for everyone, is miraculously unfair.

Emma received OT twice a week and speech once a week for the next year, on top of seeing a Cheryl twice a week. We did a lot of driving that year, going to various therapies four days a week. It felt like Emma and I spent much of that year in the car. My mother-in-law taught me how to knit, which became my new obsession. I spent so much time in waiting rooms, and it helped to have something mindless to do that kept my hands busy. Knitting fed my need to feel like I had the power to accomplish something. In contrast to the seemingly slow progress of Emma's development, I could complete a knitting project in just a few days. I churned out scarves like nobody's business. I made them for the kids, for Andrew, for relatives, for friends. I even taught another mom how to knit while waiting for our kids during therapy sessions.

It was encouraging to sit with the other moms in the OT waiting room. Several of us were on the same schedule, so we got to know each other as the weeks and months wore on. We discussed therapies, parenting, schools, siblings, family life. It was helpful to talk about a side of our lives that many did not understand. These moms understood. The needs of our kids varied, and yet still there were common denominators that brought us together. We all worried about schools and IEPs; we all experienced on some level the misunderstandings of others; we all were grieving in our own ways the loss of what we'd hoped would be.

One other mom and I got together for coffee outside of therapy. She and her husband had adopted, like us, after having biological children. We connected immediately over our experiences. She struggled with many of the same feelings I had. She was grieving the bonding process, as it was becoming more of an effort to try bonding with a child who didn't seem to care about having a relationship with her. I recognized myself in talking to her. She looked hurt, angry at times, and worn out. God knew I needed her that year.

So much of my life was consumed with Emma, so Cheryl made sure

I carved out time for doing things again that brought me joy. A year later, when Emma started preschool for the second time, Cheryl told me I was not allowed to volunteer in Emma's class. She knew that if she had not forbidden me to volunteer, I would not have otherwise given myself permission to stay out. She said Emma's time in school was my time to recharge.

CHAPTER TEN

Sinking Sanity

I was still learning a lot about attachment disorder, but it always seemed like there was more to know. Like many communities that are formed out of common experiences, there is a whole attachment community out there, and I quickly became familiar with it. Just by Googling "attachment disorder," you can be instantly connected to people who are living a similar experience. There are Web sites I visited many times to educate myself on attachment, as well as a plethora of forums or blogs—essentially online support groups—written by other parents as a means of support.

One thing I was quickly getting an education on through my experiences in the world of attachment was that in almost all cases, the first person whom the unattached child will try to destroy is the mother. These children choose her as a target for their rage. The person they most commonly use to destroy the mother is the father. They manipulate their fathers by acting sweet and innocent, all the while pointing to their mothers as the cause of their pain. Children with attachment disorder are masters at manipulation and lying, while acting pathetic to the people they are using to hurt others. This was Emma's specialty. At first she was subtle, but over time, she didn't care. Her blatant abuse was direct and in my face.

It began when my husband would come home from work. Emma

would run to the door, screaming "Daddy!" with a big smile. She'd throw her arms around him and squeeze him tight. She never looked him in the eyes, but rather looked at me with an expression that said, "See how much Daddy loves me? I'm his little angel. I love him too, but I don't love you." Andrew couldn't see her eyes to know what she was doing. She'd be in a room with him and wait until I entered. Then she'd sidle up to him, snuggle with him, and say, "Dad, you're my best daddy, *Dad*," again looking intensely into my eyes, not his. In fact, the only time Emma ever chose to make eye contact with me was when she'd done something that got her in trouble—or when she was trying to hurt me. She almost never looked at me otherwise. She'd hold out something she'd made in front of me and say, "Look what I made for you"—then she'd turn to face someone else— "*Dad*." Her eyes never left mine while she did this. It was constant. She'd do the same when grandparents were around, or friends. Anyone who was unaware, she would use to hurt me.

I'd try to look unaffected, like I didn't notice or wasn't paying attention. But all day long it would chip away at me and wear me down. After a while, it no longer helped to know that it wasn't just Emma, that many unattached kids behaved that way. It didn't matter anymore that our therapists were telling me not to take it personally. It was personal to me, and it hurt.

It didn't take long for Emma to become more direct with her attacks, and it was hard to feel so despised and hated by her. Some days I just felt wounded, and other days I felt like I wanted to hate her back. The guilt tore me up. Again, I'd ask myself, "What kind of mother am I—to feel like that?" It was such a horrible, dark feeling. I began to feel trapped, suffocated, and my thoughts became focused on escaping my life. Sometimes I wished I could get in the car, drive away, and never come back. Other days, I shamed myself for feeling that way and desperately worked to make things better. I constantly fluctuated between the two extremes. I struggled to find hope, and I cried out to God. "Please change me," I'd pray. "Help me to love, give me grace, have mercy on me."

Where is God? I asked myself. *Can He hear my prayers? Am I proving myself worthy to be heard?* But those were the wrong questions. God's willingness to listen to me couldn't be earned. I knew better even then, but the part of me that didn't believe grace was entirely true—and the shame I was heaping upon myself—didn't allow me to accept and receive what He was freely giving.

But it wasn't just me Emma was abusing. Her constant abuse toward Annie and Ben grew more sophisticated. Before long, she began using Annie to hurt Ben. Much like the way she used Andrew to get at me, she'd put her arms around Annie and say, "Annie, you're my best sister. I love you," while looking intensely into Ben's eyes. She'd draw things or make things for Annie, but wait until Ben was around to give them to her while she looked at him.

Ben, we always said, was Emma's gift of grace. Like none of us could do on a consistent basis, Ben was able to keep going back to Emma, forgiving and forgetting. I believe he loved her unconditionally. He was always encouraging her, praising her, helping her. And interestingly, next to me, he was the person she chose to single out for abuse. This makes sense if you think about attachment. Emma was afraid of intimacy. Anyone she perceived as too invested in her was not to be trusted, so she worked hard to make sure she could keep those people at arm's length. Again, this goes against what healthy people know about good relationships. Granted, true intimacy can be a little frightening for many of us. But take that fear to an abnormal extreme, and you don't have behaviors that are just avoiding, but abusive.

Annie, on the other hand, seemed to be the only one who was able to separate herself from Emma's unhealthy issues. She somehow had the ability to connect with Emma, but to remain separate from her at the same time. (This ability was my therapy goal, but I was never able to master it.) Looking back, Annie was a little example of emotional health during a time when "crazy" seemed like our new "normal."

I began to experience a side of myself I had never known existed. The constant abuse I received from Emma and watching her hurt the kids took its toll. Before having Emma, I considered myself to be fairly levelheaded. I thought of myself, for the most part, as patient, kind, and loving. I could assess my children's needs and make logical decisions. Like most mothers,

I had difficult days with the kids now and then, but life still seemed manageable and sane.

With everything going on now, it didn't take long for me to begin looking like an angry baboon. There was so much at play: emotional depletion, physical exhaustion, anxiety about what might happen next. As our children grow, we as parents become more familiar with them. We know what things set them off. We learn the signals they give us to tell us they've had enough. We know how they function on too little sleep. We know their habits, the things they get excited about, and the things that make them sad. But the longer we had Emma, the less I felt I knew about her, and therefore, the less I could predict about her behaviors. We used to say she was an onion. Each layer we'd become familiar with would reveal another layer we didn't even recognize, and that looked nothing like the last layer we'd peeled off.

I was feeling a great deal of stress, no longer able to predict what was going to happen or what outcomes might ensue. Emma's behaviors were all over the map. Things she was perfectly fine with one day would completely set her off the next. We never knew what would trigger a trauma response for her. It could be the sight of something, a smell, a texture. Her trauma responses were frightening, both for her and for us. She would turn hysterical, screaming and sweating for anywhere between fifteen minutes to an hour. Most of the time she'd dissociate, and we'd attempted to help keep her in a conscious state of mind by talking to her through the episodes. Often she'd hurt herself by pulling her hair out or scratching her skin. One of us usually had to sit by her, holding her hands so she wouldn't hurt herself, and let her scream it out. We did breathing exercises to calm her down. Most of the time we'd just wait until it passed.

These episodes were exhausting, and yet instead of Emma collapsing in exhaustion afterward, she'd shift to a hyper, almost manic state, which often lasted for the rest of the day. It wasn't until bedtime that she'd finally collapse. I drove myself crazy trying to figure out what put her in a trauma state so I could help her avoid episodes. I finally learned that her anxiety wasn't coming from a rational place, and therefore I couldn't make rational sense of it.

My responses to the unpredictability of Emma's behaviors became symptomatic. I began to feel a tightness in my chest that would well up inside me when Emma was out of sorts. The tightness at times seemed to squeeze the very breath out of me. I didn't realize it then, but when things got increasingly stressful, I would stop breathing well as a result of anxiety. Other times I felt so down about the way things were going that I didn't want to get out of bed in the morning. I began to dread each new day and yet was afraid of losing hope.

I came into Emma's room one day to tell her that her time-out was over. It had been a hard day together, and she'd stopped trying to hide her open defiance to me. When I opened her door, she had a smile on her face. I was used to that. It wasn't a genuine happy smile, but rather a sly one, and I'd seen it many times after she'd gotten in trouble. Something was different, though, about her demeanor. She was as calm as I'd ever seen her.

She didn't move a muscle as I stepped into the room. She waited until I was standing in front of her, locked eyes with me, and said, "I pooped my pants." Her eyes stayed glued to mine, waiting to see what I would do next.

"What?" I said. "You pooped your pants just now, in the last five minutes?"

Still staring intently into my eyes, she said, "Yes."

Emotionally, I tried to pull it together. Emma had been potty trained for some time now. I knew if I responded angrily, I'd be giving her exactly what she wanted. Emma often looked peaceful and genuinely happy when she knew she'd gotten the best of me. Cheryl said it gave her a sense of control. If she could get any of us mad, upset, or generally out of sorts, it reassured her that she was in control of everyone else. This was especially true if she ever saw me crying. After looking peaceful, she'd be in a hyper-gleeful state, which always made me question my own sanity. Everything about her emotional responses seemed backwards and wrong. I was coached by Cheryl to act as nonchalant and unaffected as possible when Emma did things to upset me.

In a matter-of-fact way, I said to her, "That's too bad. I guess you'll have to clean yourself up in the bathroom."

Inside I was furious. I was shaking with anger when I set up Emma in the bathroom so she could clean herself. I put her in the empty tub and laid out the wipes. Then I let her be. When I came back to check in on her, I had a bigger mess on my hands.

To her credit, she had tried to clean herself up. But there was poop everywhere. Common sense should have told me that would be the case. I was so angry I could have spit nails. Then I lost it. I began to yell at her, telling her how angry I was and that she was never to do that again. Not good. I finished cleaning her up and rinsed her down in the shower, intentionally keeping the water at a cool temperature. She didn't like that, and it gave me some satisfaction for the moment that I wasn't the only one who was unhappy.

After she got dressed, she was wired. She slid down the steps yelling "Wheee!" She ran through the house squealing with glee. I couldn't believe it. Did what just happened really happen? Didn't she just poop her pants a minute ago? Weren't we both so unhappy? Sadly, I realized I'd given Emma what she wanted. She'd really gotten to me, and I had lost it with her. I was disappointed and angry with myself, but I naively hoped we wouldn't have another incident like that one. Maybe she didn't really mean to do it; it was an accident. It could have been random.

Unfortunately, the first incident was only the beginning. Emma continued to poop her pants during time-outs, or anytime she was mad at me, for the next full year. It was amazing the control she had. She never missed the mark. She completely stopped going at random times and would hold it until she had an opportune moment. It added to the craziness. Every time after cleanup, she'd be wired, on a high.

I tried my best to maintain control, to look as unaffected as possible with little emotional expression. Some days it worked. Other days I could feel the intensity building, and I'd explode. It bothered me how inconsistent I'd become. And it was my inconsistency that perpetuated the problem. Emma didn't know when, but she knew that eventually I'd crack.

I called Cheryl twice, at the end of a couple of intensely hard days, having locked myself in my bedroom, to say that I needed her help. Both times

I was at my limit. One time I had Emma in her room, and I said, "I'm losing it. I'm afraid if I go in there, I'll do something I'll regret. I actually feel like hurting her. Please help."

She asked, "How long until Andrew gets home?"

"One hour," I said.

She responded, "That's okay that Emma's in her room. She's safer there now than with you. You need some time to pull it together. Let her be. If you can, bring her in some safe toys to play with; if you can't, it's okay. You know she's in a safe place where she can't get hurt or hurt others. You're going to be okay."

I was horrified by what was happening to me as I sat in my bedroom, feeling like I could barely breathe. There was so much about Emma's behavior that went against what I knew to be normal, and the parenting techniques we were using with her seemed backwards and so unnatural. Therapists who know attachment disorders will tell you that normal parenting does not work for unattached kids. I questioned myself all the time. "Is it *me*? Am I incapable of love? Am I crazy?"

For the first time, I realized to my core what I might be capable of. In the past I'd read articles or stories about abusive parents. I used to shake my head, unable to comprehend ever doing that. Now, I was faced with the reality that I too possessed the capacity to do such a thing. There were days when I would be wracked with guilt over what I'd imagine I wanted to do to Emma. It absolutely horrified me. I shared these things with Andrew and Cheryl from time to time, which always helped diminish the power those thoughts sometimes had over my mind.

By the end of October, Cheryl and I began discussing therapy for me to do alone. I was having such a hard time dealing with my emotions, and I didn't want to take away from Emma's therapy time. Cheryl referred me to one of her colleagues, named Linda, and I began seeing her right away. She helped validate my feelings and my experience with Emma. I needed a place where I could share what was going on at home and have someone understand.

Living with such an emotionally sick person, I was losing perspective—both about Emma and about myself. I started to lose sight of what "normal" looked like, which led me to feeling like a lunatic. My goal in therapy was to learn how to remain separate from Emma, but with connection. Linda worked with me to try to regain and maintain my perspective. We talked about parenting, ways I could separate myself from Emma when I felt myself getting too wrapped up in her issues, and anything else related to keeping our family life sane. We also talked about my emotional responses to Emma and why at times they felt so out of control.

Linda noticed, too, that even when talking about specific instances with Emma, I would stop breathing or become short of breath. I wanted to escape and be free from my grief, my anger and resentment, my self-inflicted shame, my guilt, and my overall out-of-control feelings.

The concept of grace was so disrupted, and the internal conflict I was feeling about my relationship with Emma and my relationship with God so strong, I was barely able to hang on to my faith.

Yet, I felt like the Lord was teaching me, revealing to me that the way Emma behaved with me is not unlike the way I behave with God sometimes. Like an unattached child, I am preoccupied with *my* needs, with what *I* want. I look to get my needs met with other things or relationships. When God seems distant, I need Him. When He seems to come near, I sometimes turn the other way. I can look like I love Him when others are around, at church, with other Christians, but on my own I can have trouble remembering He's there. I make choices at times that inflict self-harm. I can spend unprecedented hours worrying about my life, my future, my relationships, about what's next. All the while He's pursuing me. His love for me is forever unchanging. In Him lies the relationship that meets all my needs. He grieves with me, hurts with me, celebrates me. And yet, sometimes intimacy with Him is scary. If I really am laid bare before Him, what does that mean? And what will He ask of me? He gives and gives; my only requirement is to receive. Sometimes I reciprocate, sometimes I do not.

Through Emma, I began to see and feel for the first time what I think God experiences with me. And yet He grieves and gives and loves in a perfect way. Most importantly, He gives love that I cannot ever work hard enough to earn. Even though I'd heard that truth for years and professed it with my mouth, it didn't become an internalized *truth* until I experienced it through my relationship with Emma. Emma certainly never did anything to earn my love for her. She was my first living example of a completely nonreciprocal relationship in which I was the sole giver. Regardless of how hard I worked to demonstrate my love for her, she ultimately only had to accept and receive it. But this wasn't easy to see in the midst of the struggle. It broke my heart to be faced with the realities of my relationship with God.

Grace, as I had always known it, had become something I no longer felt I could receive or give. I only heaped more guilt upon myself. What's more, when it came to parenting Emma, I was holding myself to a perfect standard, essentially comparing my performance with God's. If He could love me, forgive me, and give me grace when I didn't deserve it, then I should have been able to do that for Emma. I know it sounds ridiculous, and looking back I can hardly believe the way I bought into the lie that I had to be perfect with Emma so that God wouldn't hold out on His grace for me. Linda had news for me. *I was not God.* I am not grace in perfect form. And my abilities to give and love are limited by my humanness. It is an obvious truth. But I was so engulfed in guilt and emotionally overwhelmed with what we were going through, I couldn't see straight.

By the end of the summer, Soni was moving out. She was going to spend the next year in Africa teaching English. We were excited for her and sad to be losing her. Fortunately, she had a friend who was looking for a place to live and interested in helping us. We met Lisa about a month before Soni moved out. She too was a great help to us, and the kids loved her. Lisa's calm confidence worked well with Emma. She lived with us until the next summer, becoming engaged later that fall to be married while living with us. We had fun talking weddings and spending time with her and her fiance, Andy. Again, I had consistent breaks that I could count on, which I believe was essential to everyone's emotional health.

That fall was a hard time for Emma. Her traumatic responses were heightened, and she was having full-blown trauma episodes at least a few times a week. We had begun to see progress over the late summer and early fall, but as Thanksgiving approached, Emma regressed. Like the year before, with so much stimulation surrounding the holidays and with our family being off our routine, Emma was out of sorts most of the time. In her struggle to feel in control, she turned up the intensity of her negative behaviors. Her defiance and directed abuse were out of control. I felt like it had become her life's mission to make me miserable. Some days I'd fight back with a vengeance, limiting and putting the kibosh on everything she did. Other days I just took the blows. Again, my inability to be consistent with her gave her the incentive to keep it up. And yet, I am human. I hurt. I get mad. I feel. Cheryl and Linda kept dishing out grace when I no longer could give it to myself or receive it from God.

My sister-in-law Lisa offered to watch Emma one full day a week so I could get a break. I usually tried to schedule my therapy sessions and anything else I had to get done on those days. Lisa and Dave kept Emma straight through dinnertime so that once a week Andrew, Annie, Ben, and I could have dinner, just the four of us. It was a much-needed respite for us, and an act of mercy on Dave and Lisa's part.

Christmas especially brought out Emma's insatiable needs. She couldn't get enough of anything. Her food obsession was high, her stomach a bottomless pit. She did anything and everything for attention, with no regard for whether the attention she received was positive or negative. On Christmas Eve, she ripped through her presents, never looking at them once she'd opened them. As soon as she ripped off the paper, she threw the gift to the floor, demanding another one. Both Andrew and I felt a sadness well up in us that we fought down for the sake of Annie and Ben during present time. It was still so obvious how empty Emma was, how desperate she was to fill that space, and yet how incapable she still was of receiving what she really needed. Once we put the kids to bed, we both broke down, feeling again the grief for Emma that she was incapable of feeling, the grief for all of us.

Emma's fourth birthday in February was much the same. Leading up to her birthday, she kept saying, "It's my birthday. I eat it." It sounded silly to hear her say that, yet it put an accurate word picture to our experience as we observed her response to her birthday. She ate it up, so to speak, in that insatiable way that was hard to ignore. I was in tears most of the day, but I managed to hold it together for a birthday dinner and presents at home in the evening.

CHAPTER ELEVEN

A Change of Scenery

It was a long winter. Minnesota winters are cold and gray. Temperatures can be below zero for days at a time. We spent almost all of our time indoors, and it was wearing on me. I can remember saying to Andrew one day, "It's been ten days and I haven't seen the sun." Having Emma indoors heightened my sense of feeling trapped inside. She didn't like it either, and she acted like a caged animal whenever we were at home.

My fantasies of leaving and never looking back had become a comfortable place for my mind to dwell, which frightened me. I knew, deep inside myself, that I wouldn't really do it—not then. But what if the day came when I really would? The thought troubled me. I became even more determined to continue in my own therapy so I could understand those feelings and work to make sure that day would never come. Andrew and I had talked in the past about moving to a milder climate, but we'd never really taken the thought seriously until that year, and winter began numerous conversations about moving to another state.

By the beginning of March, we'd made the decision to move to Colorado. Andrew's job would allow him to open an office there, and my in-laws lived out that way too. There were things to be done. We had to put the house on the market, for starters. We planned a scouting trip that spring to hunt for a place to live. Taking a long weekend, we flew into Denver and drove to an area just northeast of the city of Boulder. We drove around most of the weekend and visited three schools. We immediately liked one school and felt it would be a good fit for the kids. We met with the principal and had an opportunity to ask questions, a few in particular related to special education. We knew Emma would qualify for special education services, and we wanted to get a feel for what they could provide for her. It was clear that the school would be very willing to work with us and provide for Emma what she would need. We didn't find quite the right place to live, so we decided on renting once we moved so we could spend some time in the area before finding a house.

During the spring months, Emma was a bundle of constant anxiety. Cheryl helped us with timing, coaching us about when and how much to tell Emma about the move. Emma's confusion about what was happening was growing. I can't remember exactly what we told her, but the message we repeated to her included the basics: we were moving to a new place, and we would all be going together and would stay together once we'd moved.

By May, we'd sold the house and begun the work of packing up. Dave and Lisa threw us a good-bye party with friends from church. Neighbors threw us a party with families from the neighborhood. We wrapped up therapies with final appointments. Saying good-bye seemed rather eventful. Our therapists had worked hard; they'd invested in Emma and were devoted to helping her. Mine had helped me immensely. A simple thank-you didn't seem right. We presented a small gift to each of the therapists who'd helped us, and I added a scarf to the bag for Cheryl that I'd made for her during the many times I waited outside her office while Emma was in therapy. We took pictures and said our farewells. I'm thankful for those people who touched our lives, each in a significant way.

We were sad to say good-bye to so many friends and family, but we were also excited about moving. We knew we'd be back for holidays and for a long visit each summer. I was ready to start over, to experience a new life, in an environment where I could be anonymous for a while.

We pulled out of the driveway on July 10. Andrew drove the moving truck with his car in tow, and I drove the van. A few miles into the trip, Buddy started throwing up. A few miles later, Emma joined him. I think they were both nervous, unsure of what was happening. We'd done our

best to explain to Emma what was going on, but it was anyone's guess what she'd understood.

We spent the night in Nebraska, and we made it to our apartment by the afternoon the next day. The kids thought it was great because everything was new, and it was an adventure. Our apartment was across the parking lot from the outdoor pool, so they were in heaven. Being midsummer, it was hot, so they swam every day.

The move proved temporarily to yield a positive emotional result for Emma. Everything we had told her would happen regarding our move came true, and for a brief couple of weeks, she seemed to put a small amount of trust in us and was somewhat responsive to our attempts to connect with her. We were hopeful we'd turned a corner and the move would signify a milestone in her emotional development. Unfortunately, her improvement was short-lived, and the moments of connection vanished as quickly as they had come.

Shortly after moving in, we began to search for a church. Before leaving Minnesota, we had been in a small group with a few other couples. When they learned about our upcoming move, one of the couples mentioned that years earlier they had lived out in this area and had attended a church close by. They gave us the name, and we made a mental note to try it once we were settled.

Church had been a challenge for us once we'd had Emma. The whole first year she was with us, we never brought her to church because our therapist had discouraged us from putting her in childcare situations as we were working on attachment. The second year we tried on many occasions to bring her, but it was clear each time we picked her up that the Sunday-school teachers were having a difficult time handling her. Moreover, Emma would be out of control for the rest of the day. As in our first preschool attempt, her anxiety rocketed off the charts when she was put in a room with several other children and only one or two adults. She could never be certain she would get her needs met, and she acted out in her stress. We understood that it wasn't the Sunday-school teacher's job to be trained in working with children with special needs, and yet it was discouraging because it made it impossible for us to bring her. So for the two years before we moved, Andrew and I had alternated Sundays. One Sunday he'd go with Annie and Ben, and I'd go with them the next.

I didn't have high expectations that things would be much different in Colorado. The first Sunday we tried the church our friends had told us about, we realized it was a godsend. After meeting the woman behind the information counter, we learned that the church had a special-needs ministry. Who had ever heard of a church with a special-needs ministry? We were introduced to the woman who headed up the program, and we were elated. It was a big deal for us to think that we could begin going to church all together.

Over the next few Sundays, we brought in as much information about Emma as we could so her teachers could be informed. Emma enjoyed her class. She had the option of staying in the special-needs classroom for the whole hour or going to regular Sunday school for her age group with a paraprofessional volunteer from the special-needs ministry. We liked the idea of her being able to integrate into a regular class with one-on-one help. Unfortunately, Emma did not do well with that arrangement. They did try her in a regular classroom, but it proved to be too much for her, and the staff determined it would be best for her to stay in the special-needs room. That was fine with us. We were so thankful to be able to bring Emma with us, it didn't really matter where she was as long as she was being cared for by people who understood her needs.

While we were living in the apartment, we also began seeing a therapist I'd spoken to on the phone prior to leaving Minnesota, a specialist in attachment issues and working with children. Her name was Barb. She did in-home appointments so she could observe children in their own environment. She recognized that kids with attachment issues almost never behave out in public like they do at home. Barb began meeting with us regularly in our little apartment, coming for sessions with Emma and to counsel me as well.

After three years of going strong with therapies, I was not doing so well with Emma by the time we'd settled in after the move. Barb, like Emma's other therapists, became my advocate as well as Emma's. She did one-on-one therapy with both Emma and me, and she encouraged us to take a break from doing therapy-related things with Emma for the time being. She too helped me focus on maintaining balance in our family without all the focus being on Emma.

About a month into therapy, Barb suggested we have Emma undergo a neuropsychological evaluation. The evaluation would give us a better idea of which of Emma's behaviors were delays and which were disabilities. We agreed it would be helpful, as we were growing increasingly frustrated with Emma's inability to catch on to the things we'd been trying to teach her for years. Barb gave us a referral to a neuropsych doctor she worked with on occasion.

The evaluation was spread out over several appointments. Emma met one-on-one for a variety of tests with the doctor. We returned for a final appointment to hear the results and spend some time strategizing interventions. Barb came with us to the last appointment, and it was nice to have her support us in that way. The report was validating, but a disappointment too. Emma scored low in cognitive development and consistently fell into the "severe" category of emotional development. However, the evaluation proved to be another good piece of information we could pass on to Emma's teachers and childcare workers.

In the meantime, we met with the realtor we'd connected with in the spring. She continued to show us houses as we requested. Finally, the right place came along. It was unique. It had a view. It was private. It only had one bedroom. Really—it only had one bedroom. (It was once a garage, converted to a one-bedroom "house.") We fell in love with it anyway. Not the house, but the land on which it sat. It looked out over the mountains, felt like we were in the country, and had some breathing room. The only problem was, our family of five had to fit into a house made for one. We told the kids we'd be camping out for a while until we could do something with the house later. The kids were up for the adventure, and so were we.

Due to the size and space of our new home, we were forced to live simply, moving only the things we really needed to live. We stored the rest of our furniture and belongings in a storage garage nearby. It was refreshing, really. We spent a lot of our time outside, with the kids exploring and playing in the creek.

CHAPTER TWELVE

Upping The Ante

That summer Emma added vomiting to her artillery collection. She was still pooping her pants when she was mad at us, and vomiting was just a new way of making a statement. Like with the poop, I had never imagined she would do that on purpose. She did have a sensitive stomach sometimes, so at first I chalked it up to an upset stomach or illness. It took several times for me to notice a pattern and realize she never acted or appeared to be sick in any other way. Once we'd get her cleaned up, that would be the end of it, and as with pooping her pants, afterward she'd be in her manic "happy" state. During time-outs, she would start coughing. When we'd return to get her, she'd be covered in vomit. Once I asked her how it happened. She said, "I put my fingers in my mouth."

It took a whole year until she decided to quit. Again, she limited this behavior for use only at home, which perpetuated my constant internal question, "Am I crazy? Are we crazy?" Most people would never even imagine that a child as young and cute as Emma would ever do something like that. Before entering the world of attachment disorder, I too would have believed that a child Emma's age, especially with her low cognitive abilities, would be incapable of that kind of manipulation and control.

Emma was persistent at asking questions she already knew the answers to. All day long she would question us about things we had just said or about information she unmistakably knew. Aside from being annoying, this habit of repeatedly asking questions they know the answers to is common among attachment-disordered kids. I never realized how common until I attended a seminar led by a specialist in the field. Kids with attachment disorders often—or only—ask questions they know the answers to because it feeds their high need for control. They perceive not knowing the answers as not being in control. Emma would ask things like, "Are we having hamburgers?" while looking at her plate with a hamburger on it, or "Are we going to the park?" after I'd just announced we were going to the park. On and on this would go, every day. We had coached those who worked with Emma to say, "I only answer questions one time." Emma would often ask "What?" after hearing something, and nine times out of ten, if you asked her what it was you'd just said, she could tell you with amazing accuracy.

While we were waiting to close on the house, we registered the kids for school. We brought Emma in for testing at the district office, hoping for a good placement for preschool. She passed the tests for special-needs services with flying colors. The district referred us to a preschool that ended up being a great fit for Emma. She had a seasoned teacher who understood attachment issues, which was more than we could have hoped for. She was kind but firm, understanding that Emma needed clear boundaries with no negotiation. It took a while for Emma to feel secure enough at the preschool for her anxiety to go down, but the consistent structure her teacher provided enabled her to function and participate in classroom activities.

By fall, I was burned out and feeling depressed. Many days I would cry for no apparent reason. I forced myself out of bed each morning, dreading what the day would bring. Annie and Ben were often my only reasons to get up and get going. Preschool was three mornings a week, and due to my emotional burnout, I had terrible anxiety about having Emma alone all day on the days she didn't have school.

My mother-in-law suggested I look into a day-care situation for Emma on Tuesdays and Thursdays. At first, I didn't even allow myself to consider it. Emma would be too stressed, and besides, wasn't day care a no-no for children with attachment issues? I talked to Barb about it, and contrary to my expectations, she supported the idea. She knew I was not doing well emotionally, and it would be good for both Emma and me to have some time apart. Emma's anxiety was high either way, she said, and two days a week at that point wasn't going to do her any harm. In fact, it would be good for Emma to continue to be in situations with other kids for her social development.

It was important to find a day-care situation that would be willing to take on Emma's needs and provide care that was consistent with what we were doing at home. Through a local organization that provides assistance to families with children with special needs, we found a woman who ran a day care out of her home. She had a background in teaching and was willing to have Emma join her group on Tuesdays and Thursdays. She ran her day care a bit like a nursery school. They followed a consistent schedule each day, which was important to us. She seemed capable of handling Emma's needs and willing to provide the consistency we were looking for. I was relieved, and yet I held back on being too hopeful. I wasn't sure how Emma would do, and I worried that once she began going, her issues would prove to be too much and the day-care woman would change her mind.

To our pleasant surprise, the woman who ran the day care did a wonderful job with Emma and provided the consistency and boundaries that Emma needed. Over time, Emma eventually tried every one of her antics. Once she was comfortable there, she was aggressive toward other children, repeatedly lied to and tried to manipulate and control her day-care provider, and even became brave enough to poop her pants on a regular basis when the rules upset her. This woman handled each situation with grace and calm. I received phone calls to help solve an immediate issue only a few times during that school year, and we'd talk every so often, checking in with what was working and what wasn't, both at home and at day care.

Day care that year turned out to be a gift for all of us. I had a couple of days to myself, and twice a week, Annie and Ben had an afternoon after school with just Andrew and me. I did my best to recharge on those days, and although I continued to feel burned out when Emma was around, I told myself on the days between that I just needed to make it until the next reprieve. Knowing I would have consistent breaks allowed me to keep trying with Emma, though my efforts were far less effective than they had been, and still be available to Annie and Ben.

I am amazed at how Annie and Ben handled that time. I was available to them, but looking back, was rarely present. Most often my mind was elsewhere; I was emotionally checked out. Somehow Annie and Ben not only survived that time, they continued to thrive. I believe it was the grace of God and the help of a supportive husband that made this possible. Andrew did a great job of being very hands-on when he was home, helping me and attending to the kids in a way I was struggling to do.

The next school year, we enrolled Emma in all-day kindergarten. The all-day program went at a slower pace than half-day, and frankly, the idea of having Emma in school for a full day was appealing. The school did a terrific job of really listening to our concerns when we set goals for the IEP, and the school psychologist was willing to learn about attachment issues. It was necessary for all of us to be on the same page, because kids like Emma are masters at manipulation and lying. It's not uncommon for children with attachment issues to go to school or other places and make things up about their home life so they will appear pathetic or deprived to others. False allegations of abuse or neglect are not uncommon. The child's goal is to get everyone working against each other. Attachment-disordered children believe this is a successful way of getting their needs met. This unhealthy dynamic is called triangulation. If children are allowed to triangulate, it perpetuates their inflated perception of control, and they are unable to heal.

After a few months of kindergarten, the staff at school began to experience some of Emma's typical behaviors. They did a great job of being consistent with her, and they were on to her manipulation tactics.

By the second semester, we kept getting notices informing us that Emma was out of lunch money. The first couple of times, I thought this was strange because I remembered sending in lunch money just the week or two before. I wondered if perhaps the money had been incorrectly given to another account, maybe Annie's or Ben's. By the third time we received a notice, we called the school to ask the lunch lady about it. She printed out Emma's account for us, and we learned quickly that we'd been paying for two lunches a day for Emma for months.

We asked her about it. It turned out she had been getting "seconds" every day. We knew she wasn't finishing all her food: we'd had lunch with her at school before, and it was obvious that lunchtime was distracting for her and she ate very little, even if it was one of her favorite meals. We figured out that getting seconds for her was something fun to do. She didn't have to stay in her seat the whole time, she could go through the line again, and she could get a whole new tray of food. The rule at the time with all three kids was that they could not get seconds at school unless it was Domino's Pizza day, which was twice a month. We talked with Emma about it and impressed the rule upon her again, stressing that she was not allowed to get seconds anymore. Like any time we'd go over rules, Emma would nod her head and say okay, acting very compliant.

Kids like Emma know the rules and can recite them, but never adopt them as their own. They cannot hold the presence of rules without a parent present. So it didn't matter that we told her she could not get seconds at lunch. The moment she was back at school, the rules no longer applied. It took some detective work on our part to see that she was continuing to get seconds. We wanted to see how long she would keep it up and continue to lie about it. We eventually talked to her teacher about it, and the school was willing to have someone observe Emma at lunchtime without her knowing. At the end of each week, her teacher sent an update via e-mail about our little lunch caper.

Time and again, she continued to get seconds. To cover it up, she did what many kids like her do: something called "crazy lying." Crazy lying is telling a lie so obvious it's ridiculous or crazy, and it makes the person lied to feel crazy as a result. We asked Emma one day, "How was the burrito today at lunch?"

"Good!" she said.

"How was your second burrito?"

Without hesitating, "Good!" she said.

"Did you get seconds at school?" we asked.

"No," she said, not aware of the contradiction.

"So, your second burrito was good?"

"Yes!" she said.

"But you didn't get seconds."

"No."

Kids who crazy lie can be holding a cookie in their hands, and when you ask them where they got the cookie, they'll tell you, "I don't have any cookie." It's crazy, and like other attachment-disorder behaviors, Emma had this one down pat.

We experienced many moments of crazy lying, about everything from stealing food to what she did at school each day to made-up information she was willing to tell anyone who would listen. One day she punched a little boy in the face at school. After getting a call from the teacher at home, we asked her about it. "No, that didn't happen," she said, "I had a really good day today." Thankfully, with a school that was willing to work with us and keep us informed, Emma's ability to work everyone over was significantly minimized.

Andrew and I joined a support group for parents of children with special needs, held at our church. There were eleven of us in the group, and we met once a month. It provided an outlet for us, and although the special needs of our children varied, we shared many common experiences. Everyone understood what it was like to grieve some of the lost dreams we'd had for our children. As I'd found in the past with the moms I'd met at therapy, here too we were all experiencing living a life that few could understand. We experienced the stares and sometimes judgment from other people. We shared fears about the future: what did it hold for our children? We discussed schools, IEPs, therapies, family dynamics. Though we didn't know it at the start, God had provided this group for us at a crucial time. He knew we would need those dear people in the months to come.

Even with our breaks from Emma, the constant abuse and manipulation she directed toward the kids and myself was growing more intense by the day. As Emma grew, she became more creative in her ways of manipulation, control, and abuse. I felt to my core that she hated me, really hated and despised me. It bothered me that I wasn't able to not take it personally and just let it go. Inside I felt hurt and rejected, and I was intensely sad about it. Outwardly, I tried to protect myself emotionally from her and behave as though I was unaffected. I'm a bad actor.

The other obvious reality for us was that it was clear she still viewed Annie and Ben as a constant threat to her very existence. Therapists told us that after seeking to destroy the mother by using the father, children like Emma will turn to the mother's other children. They'll hurt them because it's another way of hurting the mother.

Emma began to describe to the kids what she was going to do to them when she thought Andrew and I weren't listening. She'd destroy things of theirs and projects they'd worked hard on. Ben received a Lego car kit for his birthday that year. It had hundreds of pieces, and he worked on it every day for a month. One morning after he'd completed it, Emma walked into his room, looked him in the eye, kicked his car, and broke it. Then without speaking, she walked out.

This kind of thing was just part of her routine. She began to say things to them like, "I don't care if you die." She'd sit behind them in the car and whisper, "I don't care about you, I don't care about you." She was constantly whispering things to them or making faces at them; it was impossible to catch all of her attacks. Amazingly, Annie and Ben rarely if ever told on her. We watched her like a hawk, and yet we knew there were a lot of things we didn't see. It didn't matter that she had consequences every time we caught her. It didn't matter if those consequences made her temporarily miserable. It was worth it to her to see us upset and the kids visibly hurt.

The crazy thing was, I still struggled with wondering why I resented her so. I felt guilty for feeling resentful and angry, and I still believed I should be able to feel *love* toward her. I understood the logic. We are wired for relationships, and for relationships to be reciprocal. We aren't supposed to love people who hurt our kids. And as parents, our job is to protect and defend our children. Emotionally, however, the logic made no sense. I couldn't accept my resentful feelings or give myself permission to feel them.

Good mothers don't resent their kids, I'd tell myself.

We saw a shift in Emma as she began to manipulate less and be openly defiant more. She no longer tried to act surprised when she got in trouble, hide what she was doing, or be sneaky. She didn't have any regard for my words (or for my very existence, for that matter), and she made it clear to me in an open, unfiltered way that she didn't care.

We took turns every night at dinner sharing about our day. The only rule was that if you weren't the one sharing, you had to sit quietly listening until your turn. This was the only way to ensure that everyone would have an opportunity to speak and be heard. We learned quickly to have Emma go last. If she was the last one to share, she did very well at sitting and listening while waiting for her turn. If she was the first to go, as soon as her turn was over, she would sabotage everyone else by interrupting, chewing loudly, and dropping things on the floor.

Eventually, even making her wait until last ceased to work. It reached a point where whenever it was my turn, whether I was first or fourth, Emma would begin talking. She'd start talking about anything and everything she could think of, right over my voice. We'd send her away until my turn was over, but she was making the statement to me night after night that I didn't matter to her, didn't exist to her. It seemed like she was growing increasingly frustrated: I wasn't getting the message that she didn't want a relationship with me, and she needed to make it more direct, more clear.

One particular night, she really got the best of me. It was my turn to talk, and Emma was going strong. Suddenly, as told by Andrew and the kids, I picked up Emma's sippy cup and threw it as hard as I could across the room. According to Annie, the cup landed in the pot of tomatoes I had in the living room. I was in such a state of rage, I only vaguely remember doing that. It was silent for a second afterward as Andrew, Annie, and Ben tried to conceal their surprise and laughter; it was out of character for me to do something like that. Even Emma was quiet, unsure of what my action meant. I immediately burst into tears, and the moment they realized it wasn't a joke, Andrew, Annie, and Ben came around me. I just sat there and sobbed. To this day, the kids still remind me of the sippy cup story, and I'm sure it's one they won't forget.

Emma began coughing that year. It started as attention-seeking behavior. However, like other behaviors, she used it only at opportune times. When she didn't know what to say or do, she'd cough. When she didn't want to listen to me, she'd cough. Some days she'd cough literally for hours, until her throat was so irritated she really *couldn't stop* coughing. She was never fighting a true illness during her "coughing spells," but again, my inability to be consistent with her got a reaction from me now and then, and that was enough to keep her going. I never ceased to marvel at her staying power.

Emma lost all regard for anything I said to her. If I told her to get her shoes on for school, she would lock eyes with me, slowly fold her arms, and stand firm in one place. She did it with everything. Anything I asked or told her to do would result in open, clear defiance. There was nothing she was willing to do if she knew it was what I wanted, and the consequences didn't seem to matter to her. Rides to and from school were terrible, with her screaming or arguing, and Annie and Ben shut down and silent. After school, the moment she'd get in the car, she'd start in. She'd argue with the kids about their news. If Ben said, "Today we had art," she'd say, "No, you didn't, Ben." They were inane arguments for no reason other than to argue. And even though she'd been successfully able to buckle her own seat belt for over a year, before and after school she'd suddenly lose the capacity to do so. It drove us crazy. It was no wonder Annie and Ben didn't want to come home from school anymore.

It took a lot of creativity to stay one step ahead of Emma's game. She still played mind games with us, sabotaging good things, then saying, "I don't like that anyway" in order to keep from feeling hurt about not getting the good thing. It was a way of protecting herself, but it was exhausting and strange.

CHAPTER THIRTEEN

God, Have Mercy

We were entering into our fifth year with Emma. My prayer time turned into literal crying-out sessions. Many nights I talked to God through my tears and cried myself to sleep. My heart ached; my chest felt tight. I was physically and emotionally depleted and felt I had nothing left to give to Emma. Moreover, I no longer *wanted* to give to her, and that was the worst part of all. I was consumed by the feeling of how sad it was for her that she no longer had a mother who wanted to give her good things. I couldn't help but project onto her my own feelings of rejection and sadness. It tore me up inside.

I laid my heart before God again and again, broken and raw. I stopped asking God to heal Emma. I kept asking, pleading with Him, to change *me*. I asked God to do a miracle in my heart. I desperately wanted to give Emma what she needed, but I had reached a point where I felt incapable. My heart was in a constant state of hurt, grief, resentment, and anger. I grieved the realization of my own inability to let that go terribly. After all, I was Emma's mother, and giving her what she needed was my job. I still felt a responsibility to "fix" Emma, to be her pathway to healing. Logically I knew it wasn't my sole responsibility, but emotionally it was what I still believed.

I repeatedly asked, "Lord, will you change me so that I can do this for Emma?" I begged God to change my heart in a drastic, miraculous way.

And if not, I began to add, "Please provide for her someone who can."

I was afraid to ask that of God, and at the same time, afraid not to. I didn't want Emma to be "stuck" with us—namely, with me, a mother who felt unable to change or move forward. And yet, I feared God's answer. What if He really did provide someone else for Emma? Would she be able to handle losing another family? Would I be able to give her up?

It took months for me to voice my concerns to Andrew. I hadn't been ready to admit that I no longer felt capable of giving to Emma until now. I had reached an all-time low.

His initial response, like mine had always been, was to think of what more we could do. There had to be something: more therapies, other types of interventions, more work at home with Emma. I didn't know how to tell him that I wasn't sure that was the answer this time. We both agreed we needed to talk to someone about it.

Through the help of a new therapist who worked with family systems, Andrew and I were not only able to voice our concerns, but Annie and Ben were also given an opportunity to share how they were feeling. For several months they had been showing increased signs of intense stress and anxiety, both at home and at school. Annie was not sleeping at night, sometimes sobbing uncontrollably for hours, and Ben was checked out at school. Neither one of them wanted to be at home anymore. It was sad to realize how much they struggled with the chaos that was so present in our home life. They no longer felt safe at home, and like us, they were unable to predict Emma's behaviors. They were in a continual state of anxiety, worried about what might happen next. The constant abuse Emma directed toward them was becoming almost too much to bear.

Over the course of several meetings, our therapist, Judy, was able to express to us the severity of the emotional state of Annie and Ben. We knew that living with Emma was stressful, but we hadn't fully realized how unsafe they were or how difficult it was for them to cope. Emma wasn't thriving either, Judy said, a reality we'd not been able to accept until now. In many ways we were living in denial, due to continued hope that Emma was making progress. She *was* making progress—physically, academically, in her ability to manage anxiety related to trauma. Emotionally, however, she hadn't made progress in the area of attachment.

As we'd been told before, Emma lacked the presence of conscience, and in the dynamic of our family, with other young children, Emma was unable to form attachments and bond. Moreover, her abuse toward Annie and Ben was only going to get worse. As Emma continued to grow and become more able, her ability to be a danger to Annie and Ben would only intensify and grow increasingly severe.

Annie and Ben are vulnerable now, Judy said, and should be considered even more at risk when they are unsuspecting, for example, when they are asleep. Children who lack the development of conscience can be frighteningly dangerous. They can look you in the eye one day and say, "I love you," then kill you the next day in your sleep because they place no value on life or relationships. Anything that stands in the way of getting what they want is a threat and must be destroyed.

Continuing on the way we'd been doing things was not an option. Emma was not thriving. As long as she had siblings close in age whom she viewed as competition and a threat, she would not be able to make progress emotionally. Our family as a unit was falling apart. Annie and Ben were really suffering. Their safety and security was severely compromised. What were we going to do about it?

Andrew and I spent a lot of time thinking and talking about what our responsibilities were as parents and what action could be taken that was in the best interest of all three children. It was our job to protect Annie and Ben, and equally important, to encourage Emma's ability to thrive.

We had two options. We'd pushed Emma for so long to bond with us and be emotionally connected that she didn't feel safe with us, and she always felt threatened by Annie and Ben. One option was to pull away emotionally. Take all attachment work off the table and, in a sense, separate ourselves from Emma. Provide for her in a matter-of-fact way, treating her almost like a boarder in our home. In essence, we would shift from a parent-child relationship to a caregiving relationship that was more "goods-and-services" oriented. The hope was that if Emma no longer felt the pressure to connect and bond, she would feel less threatened and therefore not have to try so hard with her destructive and abusive behaviors to send the message that she didn't want a relationship with us.

The other option was relinquishment. Protect Annie and Ben by making our home a safe place once again, and provide for Emma a setting where she could have the best chance of thriving emotionally—ideally one that did not have other young children in the home. Relinquishment to the state was not an option for us. We wouldn't even consider relinquishing Emma unless we could know for sure where she was going and that she would be placed immediately with another family who understood her special needs and was willing to take them on.

Over the course of many weeks, we talked at length about these options with each other and with Judy. Everything about both options seemed wrong. Would we really be able to distance ourselves emotionally from Emma almost completely and treat her like a boarder in our home? After all the investment and effort we'd put into her, we weren't sure we could ever achieve that state of mind. What was more, could we ask that of Annie and Ben? It seemed a wrong thing to teach them. Like most parents, we'd tried to model for them and instruct them in ways to care for others. We'd spent the past five years being so invested in Emma, emotionally, physically, therapeutically. How would we now tell them they were no longer to be invested in Emma in those ways? It seemed cruel, not just to Emma, but to Annie and Ben too.

The positive side of withdrawing emotionally from Emma was that she wouldn't be uprooted and lose another family. It broke my heart to think about doing that to her again. Would she ever learn how to trust if we did? What would that teach all three of the children about commitment and family? Could I live with myself, feeling like we'd failed Emma and our family of five? Could we face our community again, after all their support and prayers? Was relinquishing Emma giving up? Or could we really give her up in love, hoping she could experience connection and love from someone else?

I continued to struggle with feelings of failure. I felt like we'd failed Emma somehow, and the rest of the family too. Judy understood that I felt that way, and she said something I'll never forget. She said, "The people who failed Emma live in Thailand. You've done nothing but love her and help her to heal."

I needed to hear that like I needed my next breath. She was right. I really had only wanted the best for Emma—for all of us.

CHAPTER FOURTEEN

Show Us The Way

A s we discussed making a major change, I began for the first time to understand how much I truly loved Emma and wanted her to bond and attach. I also began to understand that, as much as I had wanted her to bond with *me*, if she was going to have a chance to experience true connection, it wasn't going to get to *be* me, and that reality was a sad pill to swallow. I realized for the first time what real love and sacrifice for Emma might mean, and it filled me with fear.

At the same time, the new *feelings* of love I had for Emma seemed to wash over me like a flood of relief. I *did love her*, and I could *feel* it, for the first time in years. I thank God even to this day that He allowed me to experience that while she was still with us. It sounds strange, but I had lost the capacity to believe that I was capable of loving Emma anymore, and that loss was a grief I carried around with me like a heavy weight. To finally feel love for her was liberating and a reminder to me that I was capable of loving Emma. I didn't want to hurt her or cause her any more emotional pain. I cared deeply about what was best for her. I still wanted to do anything to help her.

After a while, as the weight of the decision grew, I began to add the support of our extended family as a footnote to my ongoing prayer request. I prayed, "Lord, whatever it is You would have us do, we will do it. We will go either way as long as it's Your will, even if those around us do not understand and do not support our decision…but," I eventually added, "if You want to throw in a family member or two to come alongside us with support, I would *really* appreciate it."

God answered that prayer almost immediately. Our extended family came around us with support and love. They began to pray too, covering the many aspects of our decision and everything surrounding it. Through our family and friends, we also got connected to other people and *their* networks of family and friends who had either gone through something similar or who could offer wise counsel via e-mails or phone calls, based on their professional or personal experience. These people too, although we'd never met in person, were valuable resources to us, and we appreciated the time they took to help people they didn't know who were in need.

It took time, but eventually it became clear to us what we should do. In the end, the right decision for all of us was relinquishment. As much as the process of coming to that decision was heartbreaking, God gave us a peace that passed our understanding in the midst of much grief.

Our close friends and our support group from church knew about our decision, and they came around us in amazing ways. After a particularly emotional meeting with Judy, we met with our support group. We were overwhelmed by the sadness we were feeling about letting Emma go and about protecting Annie and Ben. It felt like we had to choose between our children, and it was breaking our hearts.

The group listened that night while we struggled to talk through our tears. They came around us and covered us in prayer, each one praying specifically for an aspect of what we were going through. I hadn't felt so nurtured and cared for since we'd moved to Colorado, and I felt a sense of exhaustion and relief after our meeting. They sent e-mails and continued to pray. Like our families, many of our close friends had known of our struggles from the beginning. They were the ones who had been standing by us, and to them, the fact that we'd arrived at this difficult place didn't come as a huge surprise.

We found an adoption agency in Ohio that at the time handled adoptions as well as adoption disruptions. We contacted them, requesting information about their services. It was hard not to be emotional on the phone. Requesting information about their disruption program made something that had seemed so unimaginable suddenly seem very real. Andrew spoke through tears to the social worker on the other line.

At a moment when our self-condemnation was at its highest, the agency surprised us with responses full of understanding and compassion. They sent us their printed information days later, and upon reading it, we learned that the agency believed that in most disruption cases, bad parents are not at fault. Rather, bad matches can happen. By the time families contact the agency, they are out of options and view disruption as a last resort. What a relief it was for us to feel understood.

We started the process by sending the agency any and all information regarding Emma. Legal documents, therapy assessments and evaluations, my therapy notes, IEPs. The agency had a network of families waiting to adopt children with needs like Emma's who were coming out of disruption situations. They would do their best to find a match family for Emma based on the information we'd sent and Emma's needs. They were passionate about adoptive parents being as informed as possible about these kids so their expectations would match the realities of the child. Once a matching family was found, Andrew and I would have the ultimate say by either approving or rejecting the match. We were thankful for the opportunity to be involved in the process in this way. So much of it felt out of our control, and it was comforting on some level to feel like we could contribute in finding the best we could for Emma.

We continued to meet with Judy throughout the process. She was a listening ear, her office my safe place where I could cry and talk through the pain. She also prepared us for each step and for what we might feel in the weeks and months to come. She helped us to understand that alongside the sadness about Emma leaving, there would be relief—and that both feelings would be true and right. Emma's presence in our home had created so much chaos through the years; it made sense that there would be relief and peace with her gone. Judy encouraged us to embrace and accept our feelings and not to feel guilt over our own relief. She helped prepare Annie and Ben too, by explaining the process of relinquishment in ways they could understand. She gave us all permission to feel what came, allowing us to begin the process of healing.

Before this whole ordeal began, we had planned an extended vacation over the summer to Minnesota to visit family and friends and spend time at a family cabin in Wisconsin. Judy was supportive of us going, and we knew we could reach her if needed. We were in northern Minnesota with my extended family when we received the call from the agency saying they had found a potential match family for Emma. Though we'd been waiting to hear from them, the call came at an unexpected time.

There was so much information at first that it was difficult to absorb it. Andrew took the call. Tears streamed down his face as he listened to the social worker describe the potential family. Overcome with emotion, he couldn't speak for several minutes after the call.

The agency would e-mail us the potential family's home study for review. We could set up a phone interview, and it would then be in our hands to make a decision.

If there was ever a time we needed God's leading, it was then. We prayed fervently that God would show us the way. We prayed that He would make it clear to us if this was the right family for Emma. From what the social worker described, the situation sounded like an answer to our prayers. And yet the sadness of it all was hard to contain. We both felt that day like our grief would somehow swallow us whole.

Judy had advised us not to talk to Annie and Ben about what was happening until we had received information about a match family for Emma. Before we left town, she'd helped us with what to say when the time was right.

We set aside a couple of hours to talk with Annie and Ben alone. Essentially, we told the kids that Emma would be leaving our home. We'd made the decision after much thought, prayer, and guidance. They were not responsible for Emma's leaving. It was our decision, and we had made it because it was in the best interest of everyone's needs, including Emma's.

It was an emotional conversation with a lot of tears. The kids had questions. Where was Emma going? What would happen to her? Would they get to see her again? Some questions we did not yet have answers to, but we assured the kids that as we moved forward, we would keep them informed.

As much as Emma had been difficult to live with, we all loved her in our own ways. The kids, like us, imagined themselves in her shoes. They were worried about her. Would she be okay? Would she be scared? Would she be sad? We had talked a lot through the years with them about Emma's issues, and they understood to some degree that it was very possible Emma would not be sad about leaving us. They had experienced first-hand Emma's clear message to us that she did not want a relationship. They had seen her in every situation, with strangers, with other family and friends. Emma's relationship to them all was unattached, like it was with us. And yet still, it seemed impossible to grasp the thinking of a mind so unhealthy.

A couple of weeks later, back in Colorado, we had Judy review the potential family's home study. Her opinion and expertise were important to us as we considered Emma's new family. She reviewed the paperwork with us in the office. Together, we discussed reasons why we felt like this could be a good match for Emma's needs. There were no red flags, and we agreed there were many positives to choosing this family as a match.

After a phone interview, facilitated by the social worker from the agency, and the feeling of peace we were experiencing about the match family, we approved the match. It would only be a matter of time until we'd be given a date to transfer Emma to Ohio to meet her new family.

While we waited for news from the agency of a transfer date, phone calls and e-mails were coming in from family and friends. Each offered a word of support or encouragement; some sent on verses from scripture that reminded us we weren't going through this alone. Most meaningful were the e-mails telling us that we were being lifted up in prayer. The whole process of coming to the decision to relinquish, working out the details of making that happen, grieving, and fearing had been a lonely one. Often I had to fight fear of moving ahead. I didn't know what the future held, and I struggled at times with trusting God at all to get us through it. Many times my prayer was, "Lord, I believe, help my unbelief!"(Mark 9:24). Now, not only were people close to us praying, but many had shared our story with their circles of friends and requested additional prayer for us. What a gift.

As we approached the end of the summer, I began to feel anxious and afraid for Emma. How would she say good-bye? A friend from our support group wrote, "Even though there will be some relief in letting go of Emma, you have loved her to the best of your ability, and there is great sorrow in walking away. I know that you already know this, but this is all out of your hands now. The only peace is surrender—letting God manage the things that we cannot. Emma's life is in God's hands now—it couldn't be in any better place. Don't forget that you are making this decision based on prayer and that God is requiring faith from you—to act out in a way that is totally unnatural, that defies everything you feel, believe, and know to be true about yourself. The peace can only come with trust in God and the big picture that you know to be true but cannot see."

CHAPTER FIFTEEN

Good-bye

The week before school started, the agency called and gave us a transfer date. Emma would leave us on the upcoming weekend. Time was suddenly short. We arranged for childcare for Annie and Ben. School was starting up the next Monday, so we would be back in town just in time for Annie and Ben's first day.

There was a lot to be done. We began the task of packing up Emma's things, essentially packing up the symbols of her life with us. It was a heart-wrenching time, and the two days we spent packing were spent in tears. It was one thing to pack up her toys, her clothes, her books. It was another to pack up her keepsakes, the things that seemed to represent the fact she had been part of us, a member of our family. Her Christmas stocking with her name on it, ornaments, a handmade quilt made for her after her arrival: these were the things that brought on so much sadness.

We wanted to ship the majority of Emma's things early enough so her new family would have a chance to unpack some of them before she got there. We wanted Emma to see things familiar to her when she got to her new house. As we packed our own things to go, I couldn't help but think back to a time five years earlier when the packing to leave had felt like a party. What a contrast it was to be packing for this trip.

Emma still did not know at this point what was happening. We did all the packing during her quiet time and after bedtime at night. On the advice of our therapist, we had not told her yet. It sounds strange, but Judy reminded us that for kids like Emma, all people are replaceable. Once she figured out what she was going to get out of the deal, she'd probably be fine. The sooner we told her, the more opportunities she would take to make a bad situation worse. Emma, we were told, would likely do anything and everything to make everyone miserable once she knew she was leaving. We had to remember that she was unattached, and the news of her moving would not be devastating to her.

I was anxious all week. I took time to journal my thoughts. I wanted to be able to remember this time, what it was like, how it felt.

8/10/07. We'll take Emma to Ohio a week from today. As the past several months have been, this upcoming week is a culmination of fear, sadness, relief, and hope. Emma will likely never know how much I have deeply loved her and how much I have been deeply hurt by her. It is difficult for me to put into words how hard it's been to love her, yet feel desperate to love and be loved by her—to give love in the way I know how to love, and to try and receive from her the only way she knows how to give. I feel the loss of many things, and at the same time feel as though we've been given so much. God in His mercy has granted us all another chance, and it is so undeserved. Again, it is our experiences with Emma and her very existence that are blatant statements of grace. It feels as though He is breathing life anew into all of us again.

8/12/07. We arrived home tonight [from Minnesota] and the upcoming week is weighing heavy on my heart. It's hard to be here, and I think packing up Emma's things will be a challenge. My emotions feel unpredictable and inconsistent. I feel sad one minute, fearful the next. Impatient and dreadful. Empty and alone. I'm afraid for Emma. I'm sad for her, I feel alone for her and scared. I'm afraid she's going to feel all of these things, and equally afraid she'll feel none of them. I'm feeling impatient about the four of us pulling together once Emma's gone. I feel the need to do that now as everyone is hurting, and yet it's just not time. I'm so fearful of what leaving Emma will be like, and at the same time feel so desperate to have it done. I'm ready to be done anticipating, but move on to more grieving, to healing. And yet I'm afraid to have it all happen too.

The day came to leave town. My in-laws were heading down to pick up Annie and Ben and say good-bye to Emma in the early afternoon. All morning I was a bundle of anxiety. How would she react when we told her? Would she cry, scream, cling to us? I projected onto her all the feelings I would have had in her shoes. An hour before we left for the airport, we sat Emma down and told her about what was happening and where we were going. I wrote this in my journal later that night.

8/17/07. We told Emma today that she would be leaving to live in Ohio and she would be getting a new family. We had no idea how she would react. You could say it all went textbook. Emma was excited—focused on the "new" things she was going to get— everything from her new bedroom to new grandparents and cousins. Annie, Ben, and Mom and Dad Richburg said good-bye to her. Again, everyone was sad except for Emma. It's hard to believe that in fact it is true that to Emma, people, along with everything else, are replaceable. We told her we were sorry we couldn't meet her needs. She asked a lot of questions afterward— all related to getting her needs met. "Does my new mom have snacks? Does she have toys? Where will we go to church?" We traveled most of the day—now it is after midnight and we are at the hotel. I don't know how tomorrow will go. For today, Emma was happy and excited. It was a confirmation to me that we are doing the right thing.

Emma did have questions before we flew to Ohio, but none were related to her circumstances. She never asked why, never asked when we were coming back to get her or if she would ever see us or her relatives again. As Judy had predicted, once Emma found out she was going to get what she needed, she was good to go. In fact, by the time my in-laws arrived to say good-bye, Emma threw open the door and exclaimed, "I'm going on a plane ride today! And I'm going to get a new mom!"

My mother-in-law had cried the whole way to our house, worried and scared for Emma like we had been, fearing her reaction to the news. She and my father-in-law looked in silence at Emma, dumbfounded by her reaction. They couldn't believe it, and neither could we. Emma chattered on about what was happening, making it clear she understood the events that were about to take place.

We gave my in-laws time alone with Emma to say their good-byes. Emma's excitement quickly changed the mood of overwhelming grief to unbelief. Watching them say good-bye was surreal. Then it was Annie and Ben's turn. They had each made Emma a card, and they gave her a good-bye gift of a new fishing rod and tackle box. Emma loved to fish. They took a moment to give her their card and say their last words to her. I had encouraged them to be brave, to use that moment to look Emma in the eyes and tell her good-bye and anything else they wanted to say to her. Their courage amazed me. They both cried as they took a turn looking at Emma. They told her they loved her and that they'd be praying for her every day. They hugged her and said they wished the best for her.

I had a difficult time falling asleep in the hotel that night. I cried out to God. The fear and sadness I'd had about saying good-bye was all I could think about. Even to the very end, I clung to some hope that Emma would show some sign that she cared about us, was attached to us, that leaving us affected her in some way. Judy's words came to me in that moment. She'd said, "Emma's done nothing but try to demonstrate to you in the past five years that she does not want a relationship with you." As wrong as having her leave would seem to us, it should be no surprise that she would be able to walk away.

The next morning, we spent time in the hotel before we had to be at the agency at noon. Emma took a bubble bath, and we talked again over the events of the day. She remembered everything we'd told her the day before. We presented her with some small gifts from a couple of relatives and from us. We gave her a photo book that included pictures of us and her relatives. We also put in a note from each of us: Annie, Ben, Andrew, and me. I had instructed Annie and Ben to write only what was true in their notes. They didn't have to say something like, "You were the nicest, best sister in the world."

Annie wrote:

Emma,
It's sad to see you go and we will miss you a lot. I hope you like your new home. I will always keep you in my prayers. I love you very much!
Love your sister,
Annie

Ben wrote:

Dear Emma,
I will miss you being part of our family. It is sad to see you go. I will be praying for you. I love you a lot.
Love, Ben

Finally, the note Andrew and I wrote said,

Dear Emma,
We are thankful for your life and for the time we were able to spend with you. You are loved and will be missed. We pray that you will know how much God loves you and that you will always want a relationship with Him. We will always want what is best for you and we will continue to pray for you.
We believe that M_____ is going to be a wonderful mom to you. We hope that you will be able to accept her love and that you will also be able to give her your love in return.
Jeremiah 29:11 says, "For I know the plans I have for you," says

the Lord. "They are plans for good and not for disaster, to give you a future and a hope."

We pray that you will always remember God's promise.

We love you,

Mom and Dad Richburg

Emma loved the photo book, and we read the notes to her. She loved the little gifts we'd brought from her relatives too. She kept asking, "Is that all? Are there more presents? Where are the other presents?" It was a strange experience watching her. She seemed so calm, so ready. We took some video of her talking about where we were, what we were doing, and where she was going. Even though we knew we'd never forget that moment, her words and demeanor on the video would always serve as a reminder and confirmation of how unattached she still was, and of how much we wanted to be committed to praying for her.

It was time to leave the hotel and head to the agency for the transfer. *Transfer:* the word sounds so impersonal, so unemotional, so…interestingly, unattached. "Transferring" Emma was one of the most difficult, heartbreaking experiences of our lives. We arrived at the agency on time to meet the social worker. It was a Saturday, so there was no one else in the office. We spent some time with the social worker, and she made certain that Emma understood what was happening.

Emma's new mom arrived shortly after, and we got to meet her all together. The social worker helped facilitate our introductions and the questions Emma had for her new mother. It was surreal and strange. Watching Emma was like watching a person on a game show find out what their prizes are. Emma was thrilled to find out that her new bedroom was decorated in her favorite colors, that she would get snacks, and that she would be able to take bubble baths at her new house. She was also very excited about new grandparents and new cousins. "I don't mind cousins," she said, which was true. She never had minded her cousins. They weren't people she felt she had to compete with. She was very happy to find out that she would be an only child, with no brothers or sisters. Emma's mom-to-be handled the questions perfectly. She was calm and matter-of-fact.

good-bye

We then had some time to meet with Emma's new mom alone. I'm so thankful for that. It gave us a chance to talk with her in person and go over any last details we could think of. It also gave us an opportunity to thank her and let her know that we would be praying for her and Emma.

Then it was time to say good-bye.

Emma's new mom sat in the waiting area while we went back to the room to say our last words to Emma. It was obvious we were to keep it brief and make our exit. In that moment, all of the emotion, the love, the grief, the hurt, flooded over me. I reached out to Emma and pulled her close. Looking back, it was one of the few times I can remember hugging her that she didn't pull away.

Now it was my turn to be brave. I looked my six-year-old daughter in the eyes and said, "Emma, I love you. I will always love you. I know that M_____ is going to be a wonderful mom to you. I will pray for you every day. Good-bye."

I held on to her, squeezing her tightly, as if to give her the rest of a lifetime's worth of hugs in that moment. Andrew spoke to her next. I didn't hear a thing he said, but he was crying too. For a quick moment, a look of fear flashed across Emma's face. The intensity of our sadness was confusing to her, and I think for an instant it scared her. Her eyes asked, "Am I going to be okay?"

But as soon as the worried look on her face came, it was gone. I'll never forget it. She was eating Cheetos at the time, given to her by the social worker, who said, "It's okay to be sad, Emma." In a flash, Emma's look of fear was masked with a smile. She looked at her fingers and said, "I like eating Cheetos off my fingers!"

We knew it was time to leave. The social worker allowed us one more hug. We hugged Emma for one last time. She was still smiling when we walked out of the room.

Outside the door was an isolated hallway. We stood for a moment, clinging to each other, sobbing. My heart literally felt like it was breaking in two. Emma's new mom had already been called back to the room with Emma, and since we'd said our good-byes, we were able to leave quietly alone. It was an out-of-body experience to walk out of that building knowing Emma was no longer ours. I couldn't get my mind around the fact that Emma was never coming back home—that "home" wasn't where we were.

CHAPTER SIXTEEN

Healing

With the help of Judy after the transfer, and by spending a great deal of family time together, we were able to begin the process of healing. Shortly after we said good-bye to Emma, we had to go to court for our relinquishment hearing. It was the final and necessary formality we had to go through to legally relinquish our parental rights. It was an incredibly sad experience. Our attorney prepped us for it, and Judy was there to support us and be present should the judge have any questions for her.

Andrew and I sobbed through most of our testimonies. We had a compassionate judge who, after listening to our testimony, spoke to us directly. After she had granted relinquishment, we were given the command to rise, signaling her exit. She paused before leaving, turned to face us, and said she'd read our affidavit, and it was clear we had tried every avenue to make things work with Emma and with our family. She agreed that for the sake of everyone, this had to be done. She told us to remember that all of the hard work and the things Emma had learned in our home would be going with her. Whether or not she chose to access those things in the future was up to her. Then the judge walked out.

Emma is doing well, we hear, and is enjoying her new life. I can believe that. She always did well one-on-one, and at her new home, she doesn't have to compete with anyone. We'd always said we believed that if Emma had been an only child, there still would have been challenges, but she could have thrived. Today I picture Emma coming home from school and having her mom look at her—and only her—and say, "How was your day?" And I imagine them at mealtimes, being able to talk to each other without taking turns with three other people. Without the distraction and competition of other kids, Emma's efforts to sabotage others, or even herself, have hopefully gone down. Like most kids, Emma loves talking, and she loves having undivided attention. And when she's getting it, she can be quite pleasant and sweet.

We have days when we'll talk about her, something will remind us of her, or we'll remember a story from when she was here. They're not all rosy memories, but each day I can feel the fog lifting, and my thoughts of Emma and memories of when she was here are becoming more vague. Our year of "firsts" without her was strange. Thanksgiving, our first holiday after saying good-bye, was marked by sadness. It was evident that Emma was missing that day as we were with extended family and all the cousins were together. More than anything, her absence was a reminder to us of how things with Emma had never turned out in the way we'd hoped. The dreams we'd had for our family of five no longer existed. Christmas, Emma's birthday, Mother's Day—they were bittersweet too.

Emma's presence in our home literally changed my life. Having her with us taught me many lessons. Through therapy I would not have otherwise had, I learned how to accept and embrace my feelings, no matter how dark they may sometimes seem. I realize now that fighting against how I feel just gives those feelings power to grow, and true healing can only begin when I am willing to face my own wounds, accept them, and if necessary, forgive.

There is no doubt that life with Emma was hard. It forced me to abandon all filters or cover-ups with God. I had to be real, open, bare. It also encouraged me to live in truth with others. There was no hiding the fact that I was hurting, struggling, angry at times. I wear my emotions on my sleeve, and my feelings were even more obvious during those years. I have a passion for living my life in truth, and in doing so in regards to our home

healing

life, I truly experienced what Henri Nouwen describes in his book *Can You Drink the Cup?*:

> Nothing is sweet or easy about community. Community is a fellowship of people who do not hide their joys and sorrows but make them visible to each other in a gesture of hope. In community we say: "Life is full of gains and losses, joys and sorrows, ups and downs—but we do not have to live it alone." We want to drink our cup together and thus celebrate the truth that the wounds of our individual lives, which seem intolerable when lived alone, become sources of healing when we live them as part of a fellowship of mutual care.
>
> When we dare to lift our cup and let our friends know what is in it, they will be encouraged to lift their cups and share with us their own anxiously hidden secrets. The greatest healing often takes place when we no longer feel isolated by our shame and guilt and discover that others often feel what we feel and think what we think and have the fears, apprehensions, and preoccupations we have.
>
> We need community, a community in which confession and celebration are always present together.[1]

Emma's presence gifted me with experiencing community like never before. In essence, my relationships grew deeper and more connected. I developed a level of compassion for others that hadn't existed in me before. I began to ask God for a real and genuine love for all of His people, and my heart was changed.

I experienced more than ever the act of waiting on God. Holding on, clinging to trust when it seemed at times there was no hope. I became keenly aware of the ways He was working, helping us, changing us and others around us. Many times I felt alone, and yet I never felt abandoned. God made it clear to me through the help and prayers of others that He was not leaving us. He was there beside us, caring for us, loving us, hurting too. He used other people many times to demonstrate His love and

133

mercy. I imagined at times how much He hurt for Emma. Sometimes I couldn't wrap my mind around how sad I felt for her, how angry I was for what had happened to her, how much I loved her. God's love for her goes far beyond that.

I began to understand for the first time the importance of stillness and being. Before having Emma, my life was full of things—friends, playgroups, church service, Bible studies. I took pride in filling my calendar with things to do, in being constantly busy. Through Emma, I learned that balancing my life of "doing" with time of just "being" results in a fuller, richer life. I used to feel panicked about being alone and having nothing to do. I never wanted to quiet my mind, afraid to be alone with just my thoughts. I didn't want to face my hurts or pain, or feel the discomfort of aloneness. Two years before Emma left, I began to experience being still. In stillness I found healing, comfort, and peace. It's ironic to think that the chaos we experienced with Emma is what led me to experience true inner peace for the first time.

As I mentioned before, I also gained a different understanding of my own behavior toward God and how I can be "unattached" too. He keeps coming back, pursuing me and offering me love. Because of Emma, the lesson of grace has taken on new meaning. Our family was forced to grow emotionally and in maturity in ways we never would have imagined. We learned to depend on each other, defend each other, stand strong together. Emma was meant to be with us, and we were meant to be with her.

I'd always heard that adoption is God's model of love for us. As an adopted child, I've thought at times, "Well, that's a strange model for Him to choose." Even on the best day, I can admit that it never feels *quite* right. I love my adoptive family. It's good, sometimes very good, but there is a sense at times that there is a missing piece, a feeling I find difficult to put into words. But when I think about adoption and what it really is, I begin to understand the feeling.

Adoption is a process of taking something that is broken and trying to fix it. God never intended for us to abandon our children or to have our children taken away. He created us to bond with them in an instinctive, biological way. Aside from death and things beyond human control, men break what God intended for children by sometimes abusing, neglecting, and abandoning them. When children are taken away from their biological parents, they have open wounds. Adoption is the best option we have to try and heal those wounds, hearts and minds that are broken and traumatized.

When it comes to us and God, our relationship begins broken too, except *we* are the ones who broke it. Our sin separates us from Him and is redeemed only by Jesus. Even with that, as long as we are walking the earth, our human nature will continue to get in the way of our relationship with God, keeping it from ever being perfect and whole. Until we see Him face to face, God in many ways will always be a mystery to us. There is so much about Him that we don't understand, that we do not know. Our relationship with God is not quite right yet, not even close. One day it will be perfect, and what was broken will be whole and complete. I understand now that adoption is in fact a perfect way to describe my relationship to Him.

I have Emma to thank for these things. I thought that in the end our time together would be about the things we taught Emma, how through us, God helped her to heal. What is obvious to me now is that because of Emma, I was the student, and through her I have experienced God's healing. I can only hope Emma received as much from us.

With all of our efforts, God has shown me it wasn't about what *we* did, but rather about what *He* did and can do. The truth is, if Emma's healing had occurred while she was with us, inside I would have secretly believed it was because of our hard work, perseverance, and abilities. God took the things we were counting on (our education, knowledge, and my experiences as an adopted child), none of which proved effective, and humbled us. God's message to me was, "It's not about you. It's not about what you are doing or what you know, or what you've been through. It's about what I am and can do." God knew my heart, and He had to remind me that He, not I, was in control. And He, not we, would get the glory.

I think about Emma all the time. She's one of the first things I think of when I wake, and she's always in my prayers at night. Our therapist said it would feel like a death in a way, and in a way, it does. The loss and

Emma's absence feel like a death, but of course she's very much alive, and therefore we continue to pray for her. We pray the Lord will help her let down her defenses and let her new mom in so that she can begin to attach. To love. To heal. It's her only hope of ever being able to have healthy relationships down the road, and it's her hope of understanding God and the relationship He wants to have with her.

Our relationship with God begins with us *accepting* Him. Accepting His love, His forgiveness, His grace. Until the time she left, I think Emma had yet to accept true love from anyone—to *accept* in the truest form. To receive, to trust, to depend on.

A friend said to me once, "The fact that Emma reacted so strongly tells me that she's vulnerable to being loved. It also tells me that she *knew* that you loved her, or she wouldn't have been pushing back so hard."

Maybe she's right. I hope Emma is vulnerable to being loved; after all, she's human. Our prayer is that Emma will allow herself to take the risk. We will never stop trusting, hoping, praying.

1. Nouwen, Henri J.M. *Can You Drink The Cup?,* Notre Dame, IN, Ave Maria Press. 1996.